dawn charney

verge design inc

145 marlee avenue, suite 1904
toronto, ontario M6B 3H3
t] 416 783 0265 f] 416 783 0607 e] verge@platinum1.com

MW01539614

Distributed throughout the world by:
Hearst Books International
1350 Avenue of the Americas
New York, New York 10019

Published by:
Madison Square Press
10 East 23rd Street
New York, New York 10010
Phone (212) 505-0950, Fax (212) 979-2207

International Logos and Trademarks 4
is a project of:
Supon Design Group, Inc.
International Book Division
1700 K Street, NW
Suite 400
Washington, DC 20006

Printed in Hong Kong

ACKNOWLEDGMENTS

Project & Creative Director:
Supon Phornirunlit

Jacket Designer:
Brent Almond

Book Designer:
Tom Klinedinst

Cover Illustrator:
Brent Almond

Managing Editor:
Supon Phornirunlit

Editor:
Wayne Kurie

Associate Editor:
Steve Smith

Production Manager:
Colm Owens

Associate Book Designers:
Andrew Berman, Brent Almond, Cindy Lu, Ellen Kim,
Jake Lefebure, Jason Drumheller, Jeanette Nelson,
Dujadao "Pum" Mek-aroonreung, Michael Shafer,
Maria Sese Paul, Sharisse Steber, Soung Wiser

TABLE OF CONTENTS

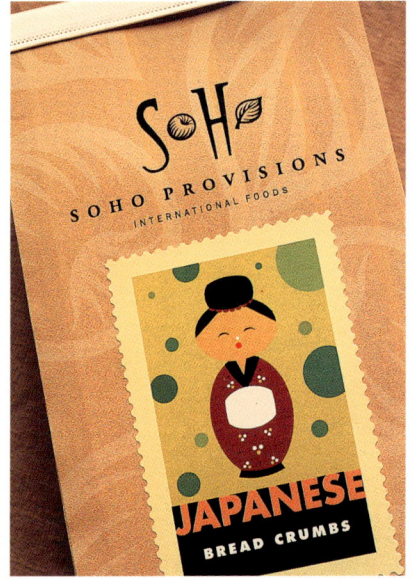

Recent Projects by
Supon Design Group

INTRODUCTION

by Supon Phornirunlit

To understand the full impact of a logo, one need only step outside and observe people. Look around and you'll see a lot of shapes, sizes, and colors; but, more often than not, you'll look at a person's face to gain some kind of impression. Indeed, logos are faces. They are expressions, appearances, sensations. If a smirk or stare reveals personality and attitude, so do the curves and hues of a company's mark. And just as a face is the most recognizable part of the body, so too is a logo the most identifiable part of a larger image. Marks represent the most lasting impression a viewer takes away from a particular company.

It is this emotional imprint that resonates so strongly. As everyone is well aware, first impressions count. The logo designer's job is to paint a picture that instantly conveys a memorable first impression, one that projects a powerful and enduring image. A mark embodies and often introduces a company's basic philosophy to the public, and this communication is pivotal to its identity. Simply put, a company had better put on an attractive face.

But a pretty face is just one part of the whole. Today's logo designs must fit into a company's overall strategy, its entire identity campaign. They must be the visual cornerstone, while still working in harmony with supporting elements. From correspondence to Web sites to packaging, businesses now have a variety of methods to communicate their message to the public. There are no firm rules governing image dissemination. Marks must carry the company's essence in a compelling manner, yet still be versatile enough to accommodate any market presence. To provide both this elasticity of image and continuity of identity is what makes a great logo design.

Today, logo designers must not only create exciting visuals, they must also bear in mind how the mark will fit into a company's overall image. A logo may function more effectively in certain contexts than others, so its deployment should be carefully considered. Will it elicit its intended response on a line of collectibles, or will this detract from its influence? Is a mark flexible enough to make an impact on more than one product? To be sure, how a logo is used can be just as critical as how good it looks.

The character of logos has also evolved. Gone are the impersonal and abstract images common in the corporate world twenty years ago. Today's marks are much more visible, and as such, reflect a more progressive, affable nature. They must hold global appeal; they must speak to a larger audience. This means capturing the lowest common denominator, provoking basic human responses in fresh and original ways. Indeed, today's visual identities are much friendlier faces— warmer, wittier, more accessible. This has presented another creative challenge for the designer: Not only must the mark be eye-catching, it must also project the company's personality—whether with elegance, humor, or cleverness—in a confident and charismatic light.

As companies and products expand, logos take on another dimension. A mark no longer symbolizes a permanent identity. It has to adapt and evolve just as the company it represents does. The targeted audience may be consistent, but the environment in which that audience lives is changing faster than ever. Today, logos and trademarks are often used to reinvent a company's identity or communicate evolving themes.

With all these rapidly changing criteria for logos, it is a wonder that designers can keep pace. This book is a tribute to those artists who have not only kept pace, but done so with exceptional style and imagination. The logos in this collection distinguish themselves for their originality, emotional content, and ingenuity, as well as their flexibility and accessibility. They all communicate an unmistakable message for their product or company, and fit smoothly within their overall identity.

As you look at these marks, keep in mind their usage. From stationery to special events to promotional brochures, all the logos displayed herein are implemented effectively within a specific context. Each communicates the central personality of its company, but always for an express purpose. As such, they represent the epitome of the modern logo—an integral part of a whole, a company's first impression. We salute these designers' ability to create such unforgettable faces.

This book, our fourth such compilation, includes work from around the globe—eighteen countries in all. It displays a true international panorama with an equally diverse spectrum of applications. Each entry featured had rigorous competition: The winning selections were chosen from over 3,000 submissions representing 36 countries. We hope these exceptional designs excite and stimulate you to consider what makes a great logo design. Readers who would like to receive more information about future competitions, events, books, etc., are encouraged to return the enclosed postcard. We encourage you to include any comments or suggestions on how we can improve our next edition.

Supon Phornirunlit is owner of Supon Design Group, Inc., where he serves as creative and art director. Since founding the company in 1988, he and his design team have earned almost 700 awards, including recognition from every major national design competition. His work and studio profile have appeared in numerous publications including Graphis, Communication Arts, Print, Step by Step, *and* How. *Supon has been recognized internationally in such publications as* Page Magazine *(Germany),* Media Delite *(Thailand), and* Asia, Inc. *(Hong Kong). Supon has served on the board of directors of the Art Directors' Club of Metropolitan Washington and is currently on the board of the Broadcast Designers' Association. Among the recognition he has received for his work are Gold Awards from both the Broadcast Designers Association and the AIGA's Baltimore Chapter. He regularly speaks and judges at various organizations and schools.*

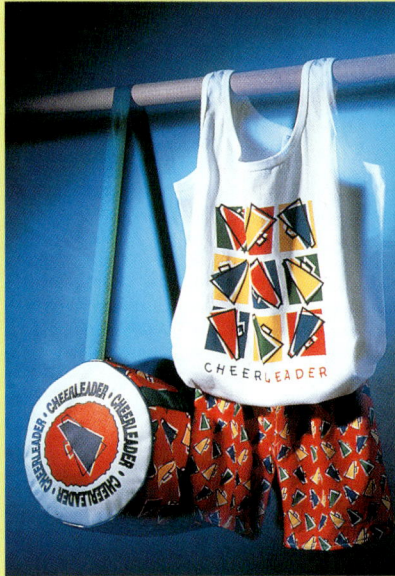

Recent Projects by
Lambert Design

SUCCESS!

by Christie Lambert Rasmussen

Developing a logo or trademark is both challenging and rewarding. Since our client companies are judged on the appearance of their identities as much as on their conduct and the products or services they offer, developing such identifiers is empowering. And what better place to start than with a new business. Its visual symbol and identity system will create the company's image. It will define who and what the company is. But first, the client and designer must determine the communication objectives together, for the logo solution will only come when all parties fully understand the characteristics and personality of the company.

As designers, we must look further than we did ten years ago. A logo must accurately communicate the client's message; this is problem solving. What type of business is it for? A retail business? A product, a service, or a corporation? How will the logo be applied, and what items must carry the logo? What's the life expectancy of the logo? Will it need to be used in different mediums? Three-dimensional, on-line, and print, for instance, all have very distinct requirements. And what about subordinate or coexisting products or departments? Will this mark have to work with other company identities? Each of these are important considerations in the development of a logo and its corresponding identity. Our answers to these questions help us form the communication objectives. From these we can create a unique image.

Today, clients have higher expectations than ever before. We no longer are designing logos just for start-up companies or for those who want to update older marks. Our clients are demanding complete identities for everything from programs, campaigns, and departments, to products and services. This is in addition to their own corporate identities. With the continued desire for more and more visuals, how does one design stand above the rest? In other words, what makes one mark better than another?

Simply put, a good idea. It's still the idea that counts. Every good logo starts with a good idea, one which captures the essence of its business. In the early 90s, logos became over-illustrative and embellished. Designers were judged on their ability to create the coolest computer stuff, instead of the most clever conceptual marks. But times are changing. We have evolved back to a preference for more conceptual, communicative marks—those that stand for something.

Everyone has their own favored process for achieving this. As for my own, I read once, conceptualize, then simplify. First, I establish a direction, then I come up with ideas (often integrating several distinct concepts), and lastly, I reduce these to their purest forms. At Lambert Design Studio, we implement this as follows. Each of us individually develops our own design ideas. We then meet as a group to discuss each option. We'll debate pros and cons, then go back to the drawing table and develop more ideas, better ideas. We may go through two or three internal rounds of creative before presenting anything to the client. When that time comes, we'll show three, sometimes four, designs from which the client picks one. What determines success? I feel that all projects are enhanced by input from several sources. Sure the solution will ultimately be the design of one person, but the influences attained through group sessions are irreplaceable.

There are a lot of good marks. These communicate a message and solve a problem; but great ones do that, and more. A truly great logo involves the viewer. It may do this through a conceptual, creative twist that captures the viewer's interest. At first glance the viewer may see the letters which form the company's initials or name, then, a few seconds later, another element may become evident. Perhaps it's a symbol which relates to the nature of the business. Such subtleties which hold our attention and remain in our memory make for great marks.

It's gratifying that clients have come to respect good work—and even to demand it. They're realizing that there is a true monetary value to our service. In fact, clients are even putting design into their own budgets. And we, as designers, are becoming business strategists, recognized not as one-time vendors, but as partners. Clients commission us to create and enhance their image.

But once a logo and identity are developed, the job is still not done. Maintaining the integrity of that mark is equally important. For a logo to be successful, it's personality must be reflected in everything the company produces. We should feel free to build off of an identity. The symbol itself, however, should be a constant. It must be instantly recognizable, a coherent impression in the eye of the viewer. Only then have we succeeded.

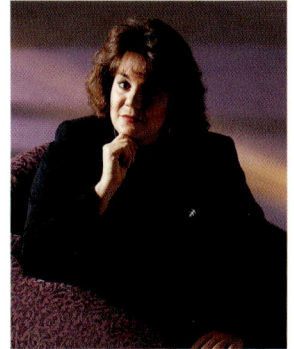

Christie Lambert Rasmussen founded the graphic design firm Lambert Design Studio one year after graduating from the University of Texas. In the past 13 years, the studio has worked with numerous ad agencies and corporate clients around the country in the development of corporate identity systems and collateral. The studio has been built on a commitment to consistently produce quality work—on time and on budget. The hard work, persistence, and determination of the staff have helped the studio produce award-winning work. Lambert Design Studio has received international recognition in publications such as Graphis, Communication Arts, Print *and* How *magazines, and numerous books. Christie lives in Dallas, Texas, with her husband Robert and dobermans Zoey and Cuervo. They enjoy weekend retreats to the country.*

Recent Projects by
Insight Design Communications

VIII

WHAT *DO* DESIGNERS DO?

by Tracy Holdeman

Logo design is one of the most important but least understood endeavors in the field of visual communication. A single image that must represent something as vast as an entire corporation is an ominous request. A great logo has to do even more. It must communicate core messages clearly, creatively, and uniquely, all in an instant, in any medium, while holding up through time. When all these factors fall into place, the visual communicators (designers, art directors, and creative thinkers) are absolutely amazing! What other profession requires someone to do so much with so little? It's like Speilberg being restricted to only three seconds for a movie, or Picasso allowed only a single brush stroke for an entire painting, or Frank Lloyd Wright limited to just one material for a complete building. It's remarkable what we do when we do it well, and even more remarkable how misunderstood what we do is to the outside world.

How do we do what we do? *What* do we do? These questions have intrigued me throughout my career, but especially since my wife and I started Insight Design Communications, and began guiding clients through the logo development process. Consequently, I've started defining what I *do* when creating a logo or trademark. My interest excludes a checklist of what a logo should be, but rather focuses on what visual communicators actually *do* when creating a logo.

I've divided the process into six sequential stages: Counselor, Detective, Philosopher, Social Scientist, Artist, and Salesperson.

1) The *Counselor* must simply define what a good logo is and should do, so the client is on the same chapter, if not the same page. This step frames the context of future discussions and makes the entire process go smoother.

2) The *Detective* gathers and uncovers information primarily concerning three areas—the company/product/service, the means of disseminating the logo/identity, and the end-user. I use a standard list of questions, but usually develop a lead that takes me off the list—like Sherlock Holmes finding a matchbox or some other insignificant clue that connects two otherwise unrelated elements. It's more like putting together a puzzle instead of making a list.

3) With imagination, intuition and discipline, the *Philosopher* consumes all the detective's information and reduces it to as succinct and relevant a message as possible. For example, I condensed the elements of Newer Technology's logo to a few factors.

The company's existing name was very appropriate because the high-tech market is evolving exponentially. Consumers demand the newest, fastest, best that the market has to offer, as long as it's reliable. The company's previous logo was a large, hand-scripted "N" which had gained equity over the years. It was worth saving in some form. Finally, rendering of the logo had to be approached conceptually, as opposed to using the newest, most amazing Photoshop techniques which would only date the logo in the future. Essentially, the criteria in this identity situation was to use the letter "n," conceptually depict "new" without looking unreliable, and avoid techniques that could be dated in the future. The Philosopher weighs and measures concepts and their relative validity to the project as a whole, in order to do the most with the least.

4) A creative imagination aids the *Social Scientist* who must develop visual concepts that effectively communicate the Philosopher's messages. All this within the elusive boundaries of society's visual vocabulary. Visual concepts have to be unique, not obscure (and a little humor rarely hurts).

5) The good *Artist* creates with relevant character and attitude. Line, texture, and shape are elements that should be consciously reasoned in order to develop an appropriate rendering style. A style comfortable to the Artist but unrelated to the Philosopher's message is counterproductive to the desired communication and only serves to weaken the effect of the logo. The Artist must be an individualist with a conscience.

6) The final challenge falls to the *Salesperson*—a quick thinker who is expected to close the deal. The Salesperson must consider the best interest of the client. In some cases compromise is the correct path, while other times stubbornness is best. If the Counselor did a good job, then a rational, mutually understood (and appreciated) solution will result. But, if reason does not work, it may become necessary to convincingly rattle off a myriad (the more, the better) of insignificant rationales to support the logo at hand. While this is not always ideal, there is hope that, with increased demand and exposure, what we do as a profession will be better understood in the future.

While waiting for the ideal future—where designers are exalted and groupies abound—you might try carrying this book around. So, when you hear *the* question, "What do you do?" hand the inquisitor this book. If nothing else, it's got some real purdy pictures.

Tracy Holdeman and his wife, Sherrie, founded Insight Design Communications in September of 1996. Tracy graduated with a Bachelor of Fine Arts from Wichita State University and began working as a production artist/illustrator that very night. Since then Tracy has developed award-winning design and illustration in almost all facets of visual communication: logos, corporate and product identity, packaging, direct mail, collateral, signage, illustration, and interactive media. His work has been recognized by Graphis, Print's Best Logos and Symbols, Print magazine, Print Casebooks, Applied Arts, Communication Arts, How, Step by Step, Graphic Design USA, Creativity, Mead Top 60, American Corporate Identity, and others. His work also appears in many books published by Rockport Publishers, Hearst Books International, Watson-Guptill Publishers, North Light Books, and Art Direction Book Company.

Recent Projects by
Viva Dolan Communications

CREATIVE AMBIVALENCE
by Frank Viva

There are certain kinds of logos which, while outside our firm's experience, interest me because they are so coveted within our industry. These are the symbols created for telecommunications giants, or large utilities, or huge petrochemical companies, or national railways. What I find peculiar about many of these marks is that the clients all want to convey the same message: They are cutting-edge, positioned for growth, and have, if not a convincing global presence, then at least a global perspective.

It's the sameness of these companies' design objectives that leads to the sameness of the solutions. Somehow we imagine that if we take a client's short list of goals and aspirations and distill it down to a single symbol—keeping in mind that, for practical reasons, it must reproduce in one color, be easy to read at all sizes, and, of course, be suitable for faxes and the Web—well, the end result does seem to be a lot of globes interrupted by speed lines and swooshes.

There was a time when this type of logo appeared fresh, even heroic. But that was because we'd never seen anything like it before—and maybe also because, at that point, people were optimistic about the future.

Leaving aside the question of how jaded we've become, the other thing I wonder about is how design firms can command such huge fees for these all-too-familiar, seen-something-like-it-before logos. I guess a big chunk of what a client pays for must be the rationale leading up to that seemingly inevitable solution—plus all the thought that goes into applying the logo on everything from trucks to lapel buttons. This high-priced thinking eventually resolves itself into a document called a corporate identity manual—adherence to which, in my experience, falls off as soon as a respectable period of time has passed. Usually about two months.

It would be simplistic to dismiss all these global-corporate logos out of hand. Some are elegant, beautifully balanced, and sensitive—a feat that's all the more admirable, given the predictability of the problems they solve. Maybe my real problem is that I lack the intellectual rigor to do endless variations, slowly polishing a few elements into a jewel with its own defensible, internal logic. In fact, it strikes me as a bit perverse that a designer would actually want to do one of these logos: pushing and pinching globes, tinkering with speed lines and swooshes until going blind. But then, I guess such jobs, in addition to paying very well, aren't actually done by a design firm's principals. Hey, wait a minute—where can I get me one of them projects?

At our firm, we approach the creation of an identity in the same way we approach that of a brochure, a catalogue, or any other piece of corporate communications. We try to get at what is different about a company or organization. What special blend of personality traits distinguishes it from other, similar ones? We look for a sense of humor, compassion, wisdom, irony, tradition, playfulness—something we can hang our hats on creatively. Every piece of communications the company issues should evoke that same feeling and attitude. The alternative is to come across as just another nameless, faceless giant with dreams of global domination.

Companies, even big ones, really do have unique personalities, histories, and mythologies. Putting aside the issue of brand equity for a moment, when a major corporation reinvents itself (as they all must from time to time), it would really be nice to see a bit of soul-searching reflected in the identity—a more human element that lets you know this company is a collection of real people, not just a big, colorless machine. That would certainly get my interest and sympathy.

In the end, though, it's really what a company does in the world that determines whether its logo is successful or not. Is it a good corporate citizen? Does it make quality merchandise? Are its products or services imaginative and useful? The Nike logo, while I like it, is not especially brilliant or original in itself. But because Nike has such an impressive track record in its marketing and product development, the logo transcends the fact that it is a swoosh/checkmark and simply means innovative, youthful, fashionable…Nike.

Similarly, the most clever thing about the revamped Federal Express identity is not the physical mark but the decision to shorten the name. Furthermore, what is evoked by that name, and what really wins my loyalty, is the reliability of the service and my positive experiences with helpful, knowledgeable FedEx staff.

Many of the logos you'll see in this book have the qualities I'm talking about: personality, quirkiness, irony, humanity. But these tend to be for small companies and individuals. I think there's an opportunity for large corporations with a lot of visibility to take a lesson from these smaller firms and create marks that are bold, fresh, even heroic—which, ironically, is how their current logos seemed when we first saw them. Before we became jaded.

Frank Viva is a partner in the Toronto firm Viva Dolan Communications and Design. A graduate in Experimental Art from the Ontario College of Art, he studied for two years in New York (where he discovered Modernism in the homes of the wealthy socialites to whom he delivered seltzer water). He wears many hats: art director, designer, illustrator, and (as if that weren't enough) president of the Advertising and Design Club of Canada. Frank's work has been recognized internationally by publications such as Communication Arts, Graphis, AIGA, The Type Directors Club, and American Illustration.

JUDGES' CHOICE

Client: Breeze Development Co. Ltd / Design Firm: Addison Design Consultants Pte Ltd

Client:
Breeze Development Co. Ltd.
Nature of Business:
Shopping mall development
Design Firm:
Addison Design Consultants Pte Ltd
Art Director:
Keith Chan

A spirited color palette enlivens this logo for a developer of shopping malls. The perfect circle combines with its artistic opposite—the sweeping brushstroke—to form this harmonious design. "It really is unique…like a fresh breeze," said one of the judges.

Breeze

Client:
Printel
Nature of Business:
Printing
Design Firm:
I.M. Studio
Art Director:
Igor Masnjak

Registration marks are hackneyed design elements in printers' logos everywhere. This one, however, is more than the sum of its parts. Both the letterform "P" and a registration mark are constructed through the precise placement of colored bars and curves. Nature's full color spectrum is represented.

JUDGES' CHOICE

Client: STAR Radio/STAR TV / Design Firm: PPA Design Ltd.

Client:
STAR Radio/STAR TV
Nature of Business:
Popular music radio station
Design Firm:
PPA Design Ltd.
Art Directors:
Byron Jacobs, Joe Kurzer
Designer:
Byron Jacobs
Illustrator:
Dennis Chan

"Spinning disks" is what DJs do so an
image of such is the perfect logo for
this Hong Kong-based radio station.
Strong, primary colors form the bor-
der of this disk and a centered "C"
is a stand-in for the station's name,
Classic Hits.

Client:
No Tomorrow
Nature of Business:
Music group
Design Firm:
Insight Design Communications
Art Directors:
Sherrie and Tracy Holdeman
Illustrators:
Sherrie and Tracy Holdeman

There is no tomorrow when a time bomb is ticking with only a few minutes left before destruction. This logo visually depicts the band's unusual appellation, but, instead of being frightening, is actually quite amusing.

JUDGES' CHOICE

Client: Trudy Prokop / Design Firm: MB Design

Client:
Trudy Prokop
Nature of Business:
Restaurant
Design Firm:
MB Design
Art Director:
Marcus Braun
Photographer:
Paul Joseph

"One of the most original marks I've seen," exclaimed one judge, "is this logo for Chives Bistro." Because of the assumed difficulty of application, very few logos are photo illustrations. For this reason, this logo stands out from the crowd of restaurant logos—even good ones.

C H I V E S
B I S T R O

Client:
Joze Lokar Foundation
Design Firm:
KROG
Art Director:
Edi Berk

In this mark for a Slovenian foundation, a cartoon-like dove represents
peace. Its dusty, smoky background
highlights the image, and suggests
a phoenix rising from the ashes.
"There is hope," is the message
behind this logo.

ZA ŽIVLJENJE

BREZ ODVISNOSTI

JUDGES' CHOICE

Client: Chips / Design Firm: Gardner Design

Client:
Chips
Nature of Business:
Computer upgrades
Design Firm:
Gardner Design
Art Director:
Bill Gardner

Reminiscent of a computer chip, or even a circuit board, this logo for a computer-upgrade company named Chips is cleverly tilted upwards. "To my eye," stated one judge, "this suggests the higher performance of upgraded systems."

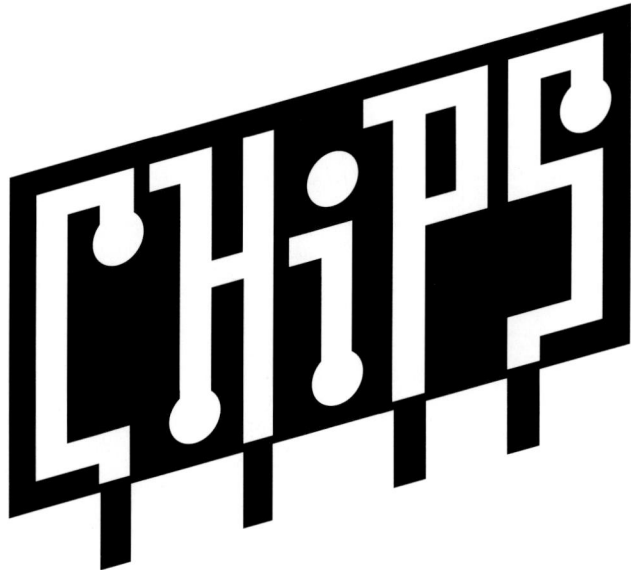

Client:
The Golden Voices of Opera
& the Canadian Pops Orchestra
Nature of Business:
Professional musicians
Design Firm:
Brown Communications Group
Art Director:
Morris Antosh
Illustrator:
Morris Antosh

Both delicate and primitive, this
logo effortlessly combines a childlike
stick figure with an elongated double
eighth note. The result is a logo
whose personality is both playful
and graceful—a perfect antidote
to the all-too-typical conservative
orchestra marks.

JUDGES' CHOICE

Client: Letterbox Design Group / Design Firm: Letterbox Design Group

Client:
Letterbox Design Group
Nature of Business:
Graphic design
Design Firm:
Letterbox Design Group
Art Director:
Kiky Kambylis
Designers:
Kiky Kambylis, Laurie Thibeault

Logos and stationery systems developed by graphic designers for their own use are often the most telling. This identity gets right down to business, rejecting all unnecessary embellishment. Our judges made particular note of the differing graphic placements (or lack thereof, in the case of the envelope) in relation to the firm's name.

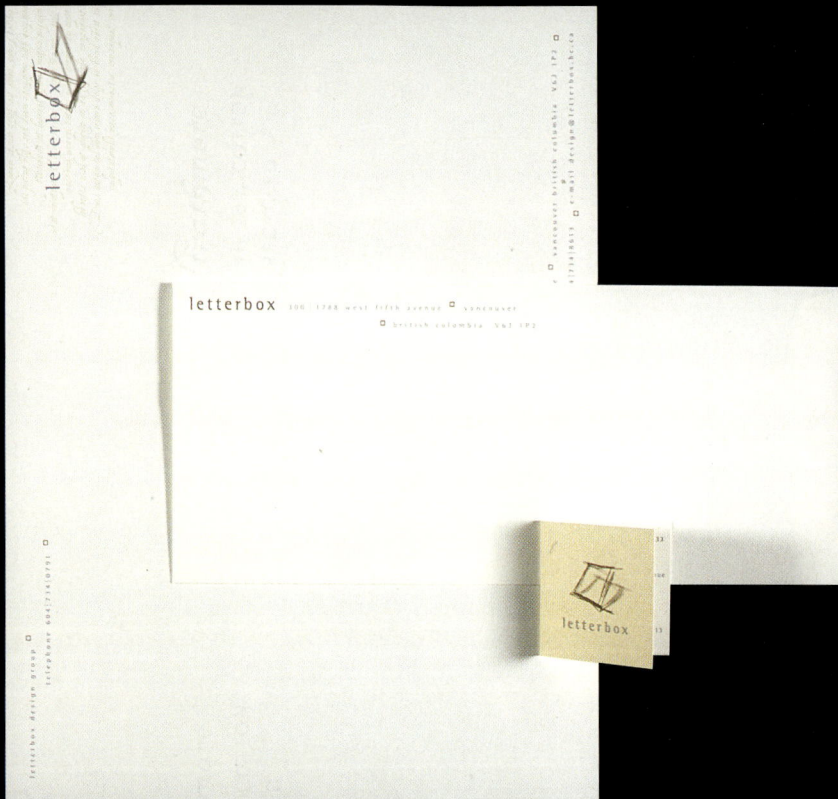

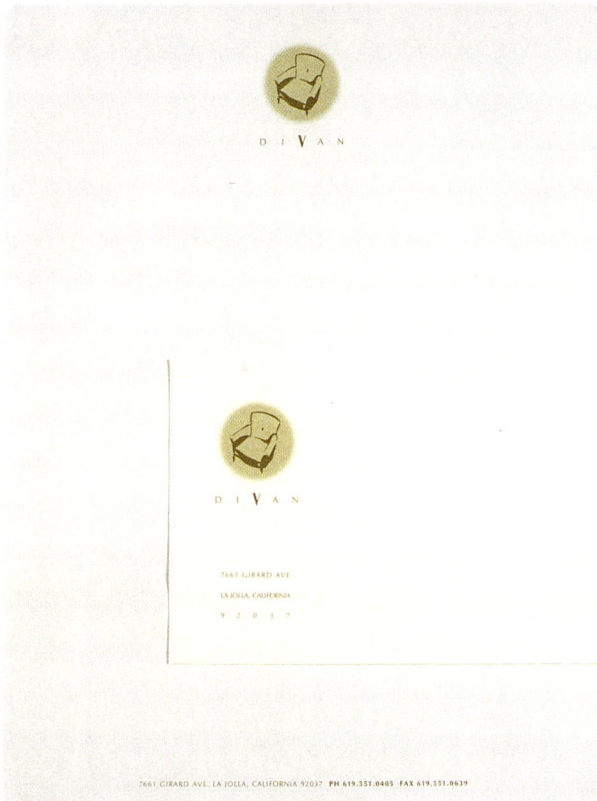

Client:
Divan Furnishings/Showroom
Nature of Business:
Furniture retail
Design Firm:
Miriello Grafico Inc.
Art Director:
Ron Miriello
Designer:
Courtney Mayer
Illustrator:
Courtney Mayer

A "divan" is typically a type of sofa, but, in the case of this logo for a furniture showroom and store, a chair suffices. The illustration works especially well surrounded by the gold, medallion-like circle. Summarized one judge: "It gives the identity a very upscale, classic look."

JUDGES' CHOICE

Client: Scott Hull Associates / Design Firm: Scott Hull Associates

Client:
Scott Hull Associates
Nature of Business:
Artist agency
Design Firm:
Scott Hull Associates
Art Director:
Lori Siebert

Such departure from stationery "rules" is permitted when your market is other designers and your client is an artist's agent. This identity—color-intensive and highly graphic—is an exciting compilation of diverse images.

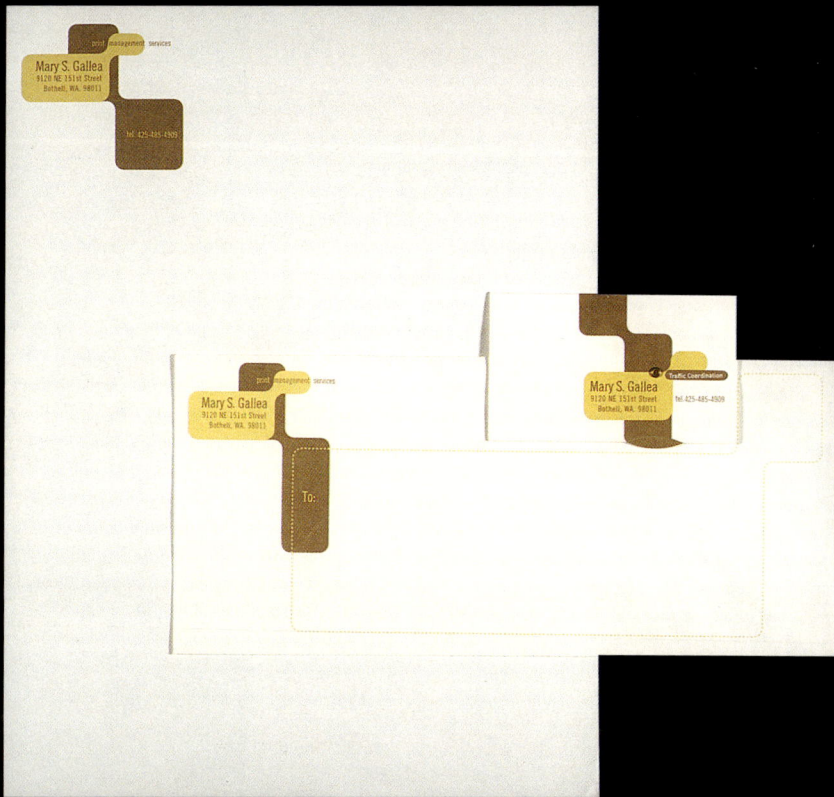

Client:
Mary Gallea
Nature of Business:
Print production
Design Firm:
Design Guys
Art Director:
Steven Sikora
Designer:
Mitch Morse

An assemblage of fluid squares characterizes this very progressive stationery package for a print-production company. Its muted color palette succeeds in balancing the otherwise hip, urban look of Mary Gallea's identity.

Client:
The Lionel Corporation
Nature of Business:
Model railroad toys
Design Firm:
Michael Stanard, Inc.
Art Directors:
Michael Stanard, Marc Fuhrman
Designer:
Marc Fuhrman

"Legendary" says it all. This elegant stationery package for the Lionel Corporation takes us back to another era, when the railways were a quintessential feature on the American landscape. The mark's use of typography is at once modern and nostalgic, almost art deco in its geometry.

Client:
Lambert Design
Nature of Business:
Design
Design Firm:
Lambert Design
Art Director:
Christie Lambert

Between the uniquely curved diecuts and the fiery colors trapping elliptical disks of black, this stationery package wants to be noticed. Its otherwise traditional look, demonstrated by black italic typography and white stock, keep it from being overdone. The back of the letterhead, by the way, is flooded with the same bright yellow as the logo's "d".

JUDGES' CHOICE

Client: Miriello Grafico Inc. / Design Firm: Miriello Grafico Inc.

Client:
Miriello Grafico Inc.
Nature of Business:
Design
Design Firm:
Miriello Grafico Inc.
Art Director:
Ron Miriello

This identity system for a graphic
design firm was meant to be intimate,
while still conveying a professional
image. Craftsmanship on this level is
not often seen: The business cards
are perforated, and contain a random
image on the reverse; the #10 envelope also features a perforation, this
time on the end, which is torn off to
access the contents.

MIKE RABE MUSIC ENGRAVING

1991 Brewster Street
Saint Paul, Minnesota 55108

612.647.6803
rabex005@tc.umn.edu

MIKE RABE MUSIC ENGRAVING

1991 Brewster Street
Saint Paul, Minnesota 55108

612.647.6803
rabex005@tc.umn.edu

Client:
Mike Rabe
Nature of Business:
Music engraving
Design Firm:
Design Guys
Art Director:
Amy Kirkpatrick

A progressive—but clean—look characterizes this identity system for a
music-engraving company. Instead of
fighting with the typography, the system of underlining and crossing rules
actually enhances it.

Client:
Pablo Work Shop
Nature of Business:
Music
Design Firm:
Design Club Inc.
Art Director:
Katsuhiro Kinoshita

The fingertips of a uncharacteristi-
cally symmetrical hand spell out the
name Pablo, with the rest of the
music company's name on the palm.
Providing a strong contrast to the
bold black and red of the hand and
name is an almost eerie, blue haze
which surrounds the image. Taken
as a whole, the mark is unique,
and, at first glance, is suggestive of a
king's crown.

EXPERTS IN
VISUAL LANGUAGE

COZZOLINO · ELLETT
DESIGN D'VISION PTY LTD

Client:
D'Vision
Nature of Business:
Graphic design
Design Firm:
Cozzolino Ellett Design D'Vision
Art Director:
Phil Ellet
Illustrator:
Jeff Fisher

This self-promotion for a graphic design firm is both friendly and professional. As one judge said, "The two waving images on the brochure's cover immediately bring the reader in and make him or her feel comfortable." This same illustration style is featured throughout, adding a personal touch, and giving the impression of a capable company that doesn't take itself too seriously.

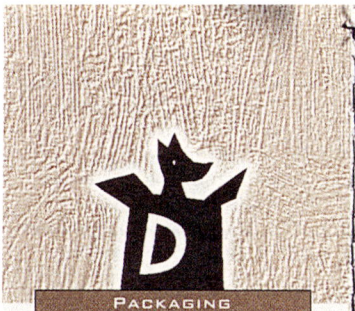

PACKAGING

Good packaging does a lot more than protect the life of the product, it should bring the product to life: firstly by drawing attention to it, then positioning it, and finally adding to and becoming part of its appeal.
For packaging to work over and over again, in the home and on the supermarket shelf, it is vital that the visual language expresses the truth of the product.

Corporate literature is like a spokesperson for an organisation. That person will not be judged simply on what they say but more on how they say it.
When the visual language of a corporation is pertinent and potent, then its corporate literature offers an engaging exploration of the character attributes and positive values of the organisation.

CORPORATE LITERATURE

JUDGES' CHOICE

Client: The Coca-Cola Company / Design Firm: SBG Enterprise

Client:
The Coca-Cola Company
Nature of Business:
Beverage production/distribution
Design Firm:
SBG Enterprise
Art Director:
Mark Bergman
Designers:
Vicki Cero, Mary Brucken

This redesigned packaging for Diet Coke (known as Coca-Cola light in some parts of the world) is both familiar and new. It retains the omnipresent Coca-Cola red, the script typography, and the bell-shaped glass—but this time the latter is rendered in a hip, almost urban style. The addition of the gas bubbles suggest both the drink's carbonation and refreshing quality.

Client: Starbucks Coffee Company / Design Firm: Hornall Anderson Design Works, Inc.

Client:
Starbucks Coffee Company
Nature of Business:
Coffee and specialty product retail
Design Firm:
Hornall Anderson Design Works, Inc.
Art Director:
Jack Anderson
Designers:
Jack Anderson, Julie Lock, Jana Nishi, Julie Keenan, Julia LaPine, Mary Chin Hutchison
Illustrator:
George Tanagi

Frappuccino is a line of sweetened, flavored coffees meant to be served over ice. Its packaging is consistent with the natural look of all Starbucks products, but with the brand's logo rendered in a light, curvy script. "It makes me want to go out and get a Frappuccino right now," exclaimed one coffee-loving judge.

Client:
Executive Risk Inc.
Nature of Business:
Reinsurance
Design Firm:
Ted Bertz Graphic Design, Inc.
Art Director:
Ted Bertz
Designers:
Ted Bertz, Mimi LaPoint
Illustrator:
David Schulz
Photographer:
Paul Horton

Its cover immediately suggests that this is not a typical annual report. From its illustrations and hot colors to its typography, this piece will be noticed. However innovative its graphics, the overall feel is still corporate, elegant, and serious—the perfect solution for a reinsurance company.

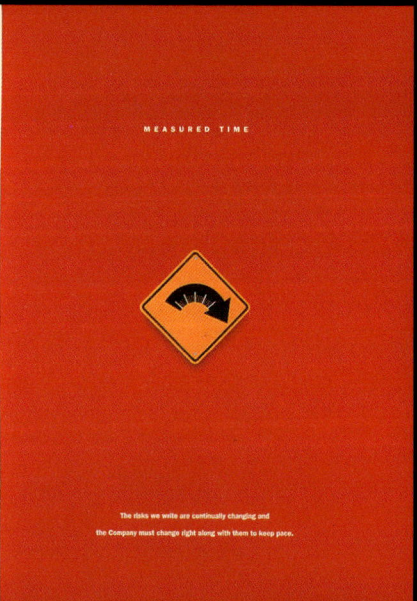

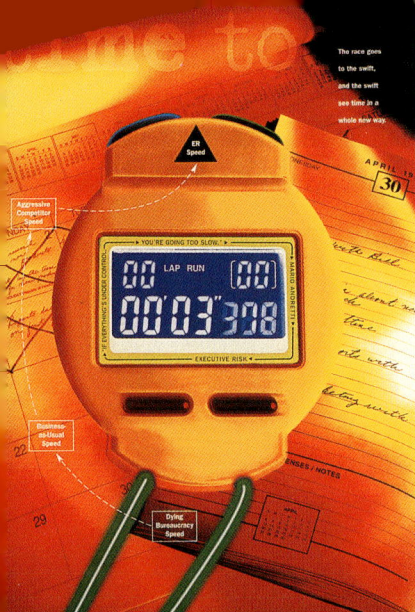

The race goes to the swift, and the swift see time in a whole new way.

"Time-shifting" is a term that was coined to describe how VCR users can tape TV broadcasts for later viewing. Executive Risk uses technology to time-shift new product innovations, but we shift it in the opposite direction. Our technology-oriented approach permits new coverages to be implemented far sooner than would have been otherwise possible. Without a formal research and development department, new product R&D constantly races along high-speed lines of internal communication, even as the product team members conduct Company business around the country and, increasingly, around the globe. As is true of our approach to business issues in general, we are committed to flexibility and "up-gradability" in our information systems. We are unburdened by any commitment to outmoded "big-box" computer centers, and we continue to develop in-house applications that speed the underwriting and policy issuance functions.

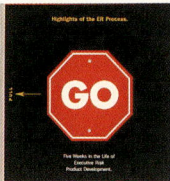

Additionally, departments within the Company are experimenting with expanded uses for our Web site, as well as with video conferencing, voice recognition systems and a paperless office environment. Our people are eagerly trying to find smarter solutions to business problems, and technology is opening up some truly exciting possibilities. This may be an area where impatience is a virtue.

Highlights of the ER Process.

GO

Five Weeks in the Life of Executive Risk Product Development.

Programs: Helping to Target our Markets

Since reducing communications gaps is a sure-fire way to optimize turnaround time without impacting quality, the Company is engaged in several efforts that effectively bring us closer to the people we serve. For example, during 1996 the commercial underwriting unit was organized into four geographic regions and three industry-specific lines. The intent is to maintain centralized risk assessment and pricing in Simsbury, a key to profitable, consistent underwriting, while increasing underwriter accessibility to the brokers and insureds with whom they work. Additionally, the Company will be adding to its growing network of program administration relationships. Program business allows Executive Risk insurance products to be brought efficiently to large groups of allied professionals.

Program administrators are independent agents who have extensive experience with errors and omissions coverage for a specified class of professionals, like psychologists. Carefully selected and screened, the administrator enters into an exclusive arrangement and receives the "pen," that is, a carefully delineated underwriting authority. Program administration is an area where our organizational agility and flexibility have created a number of exciting program opportunities for the Company and its producers. As a result of our corporate mobility, Executive Risk is now one of the country's largest issuers of errors and omissions liability insurance for psychologists. Attracting similar programs will definitely play a key role in helping us reach our goals in coming years.

SERVICE

We've targeted programs for allied professional groups as a way to diversify and grow.

Mark J. Krum
Senior Vice President

JUDGES' CHOICE

Client: American Pacific Corporation / Design Firm: White Design, Inc.

Client:
American Pacific Corporation
Nature of Business:
Specialty chemical manufacture
Design Firm:
White Design, Inc.
Art Director:
Jamie Graupner
Illustrator:
James Steinberg

Muted earth tones of browns, blues, and rusts give a warm, comforting feel to this annual report for a chemical manufacturing company. The illustrations each suggest science and research, but in a context of everyday life. The addition of sidebars throughout is a nice, unexpected touch.

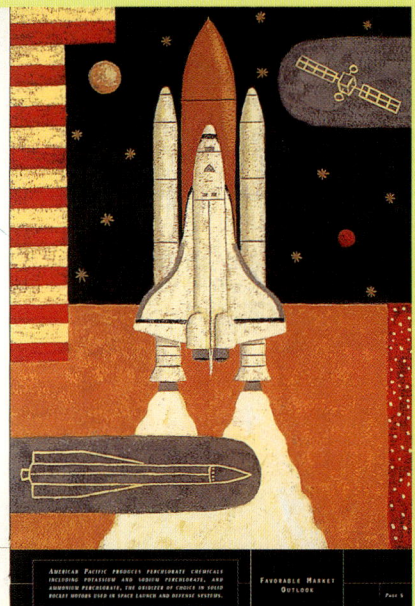

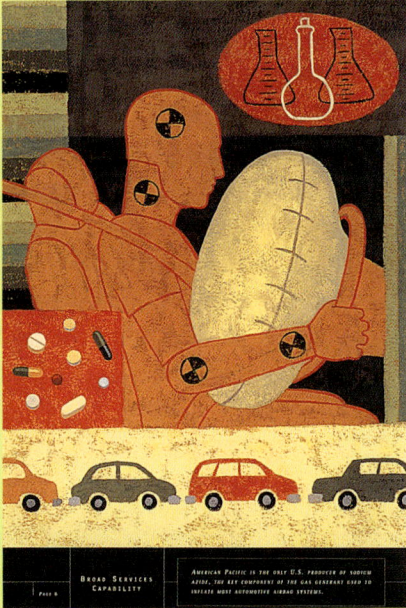

SODIUM AZIDE

SODIUM AZIDE MARKET: Demand for sodium azide is currently substantially less than supply on a worldwide basis. In addition, the Company believes that Japanese sodium azide producers have been pricing imports unlawfully. As a result of these factors, the price per pound of sodium azide has eroded over the last few years. In January 1996, the Company filed an antidumping petition respecting Japanese imports of sodium azide. In August 1996, the United States Department of Commerce issued a preliminary determination that Japanese imports of sodium azide have been sold in the United States at prices significantly below fair value. A final resolution of the antidumping issue is expected soon. The Company remains committed to being the dominant supplier of sodium azide and appears well on its way to achieving this goal.

AZIDE PERFORMANCE: The financial performance of the sodium azide operation improved substantially during fiscal 1996. Sales for the year were $12 million compared to $6.6 million in fiscal 1995. More importantly, EBITDA was $2 million this year compared to a negative EBITDA of $3.9 million during the year ended September 30, 1995. Management is pleased with the progress of the azide business and looks forward to continued improvement in fiscal 1997.

AUTOMOTIVE AIRBAG SAFETY PRODUCTS

PHARMACEUTICAL PRODUCTS

EXPLOSIVE PRODUCTS

PYROTECHNIC PRODUCTS

BROAD SERVICES CAPABILITY

American Pacific is the only U.S. producer of sodium azide, the key component of the gas generant used to inflate most automotive airbag systems.

ENVIRONMENTAL PROTECTION PRODUCTS

IMPROVED ELECTROLYTIC CELL: The introduction of our new cell has had a significant impact on this business. The new cell offers system buyers reduced power consumption and has opened up a vast potential market for the Company. The Company has focused its recent marketing efforts on this market, which consists principally of water treatment systems serving power plants and petroleum production facilities. The market seems particularly strong in the Middle East and the Asia-Pacific, with a number of new seaside utility plant projects announced for areas such as Taiwan, Malaysia and mainland China.

PERFORMANCE: Environmental protection equipment sales were $3.1 million during fiscal 1996 compared to $1.7 million last year. At September 30, 1996, the backlog for deliveries of equipment in fiscal 1997 was approximately $1.8 million. As a result of the enhanced competitive position offered by the new cell, the Company has enjoyed an increase in the bidding activity during the past year. The Company is encouraged by this increased activity and will continue its exploitation of the activities of this segment, with particular emphasis on the backlog of orders.

OIL AND GAS DRILLING AND PRODUCTION

WASTE TREATMENT FACILITIES

ODOR CONTROL

SEASIDE UTILITY PLANTS

NEW, COMPETITIVE TECHNOLOGIES

American Pacific designs and manufactures pollution abatement systems used to treat sea and waste water and control noxious odors.

MERIT AWARDS

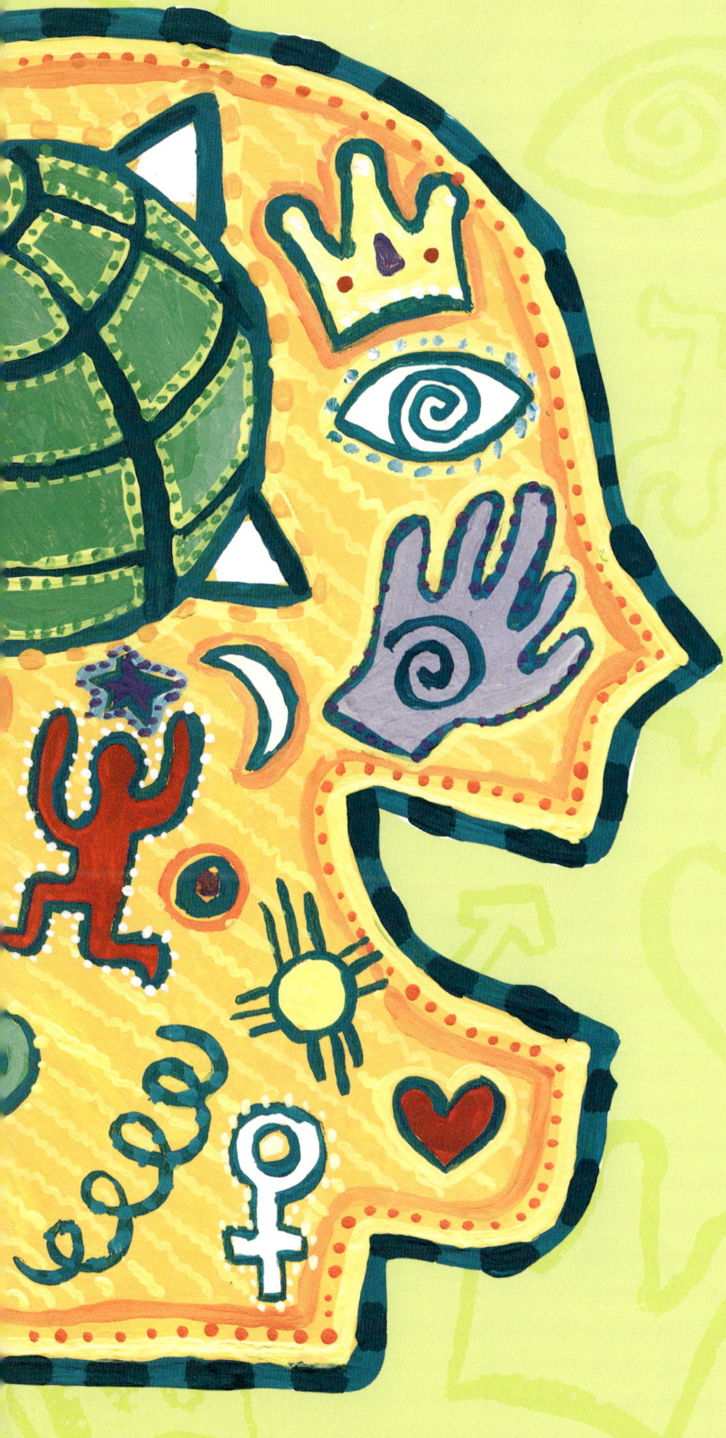

Client:
Aureal Semiconductor
Nature of Business:
Audio computer chip manufacture
Design Firm:
Diane Fous Design
Art Director:
Diane Fous
Designer:
Amornrat Vatanatumrak, Diane Fous

Client:
Aqualine Surfwear
Nature of Business:
Surf clothing production
Design Firm:
Robert Beck Design
Art Director:
Robert Beck
Illustrator:
Robert Beck

Client:
Arlux Fiber Optics System
Nature of Business:
Fiber optics installation
Design Firm:
Refinery Design Co.
Art Director:
Michael Schmalz

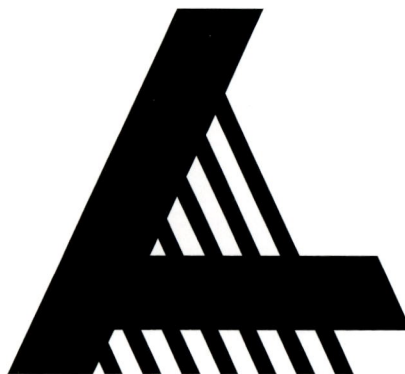

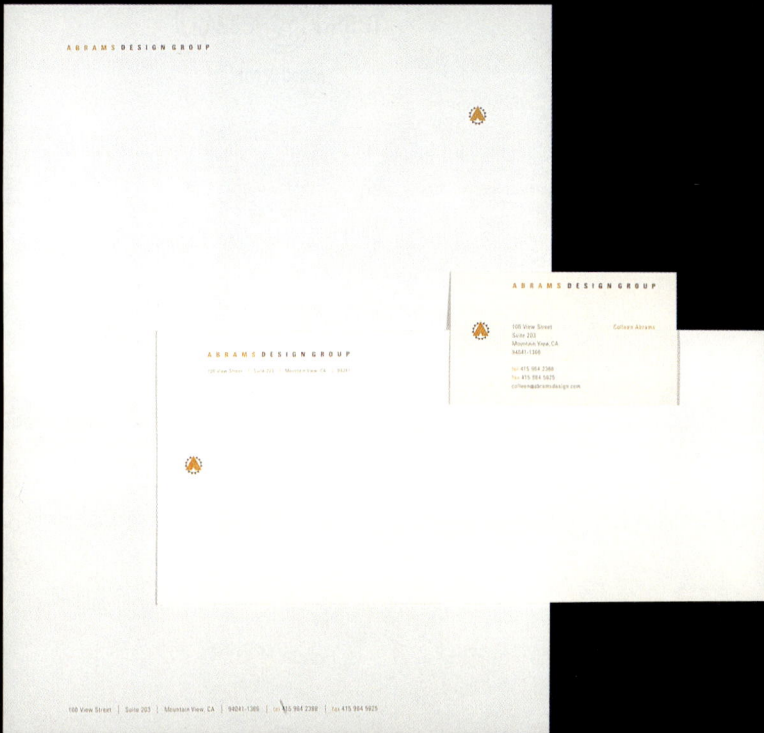

Client:
Abrams Design Group
Nature of Business:
Graphic design
Design Firm:
Abrams Design Group
Art Director:
Colleen Abrams
Designer:
Sander Leech
Illustrator:
Sander Leech

Client:
Alliage 3
Nature of Business:
Underground film production
Design Firm:
Tarzan Communications Inc.
Art Directors:
Daniel Fortin, George Fok
Designer:
Michel Valois
Illustrator:
Michel Valois

Client:
American Advertising
Nature of Business:
Direct-mail advertising
Design Firm:
Greteman Group
Art Directors:
Sonia Greteman,
James Strange

Client:
Aeroware
Nature of Business:
Computer software
Design Firm:
Swieter Design U.S.
Art Director:
John Swieter
Designer:
Julie Poth

Client:
Andrews Paint
Nature of Business:
Paint and home centers
Design Firm:
Gardner Design
Art Director:
Bill Gardner
Designers:
Bill Gardner, Mike Kasten

Client:
Atmosphone
Nature of Business:
Cellular phones
Design Firm:
Swieter Design U.S.
Art Director:
John Swieter
Designer:
Julie Poth

Client:
Animatics Interactive
Nature of Business:
Interactive multimedia
Design Firm:
Parable Communications Corp.
Art Director:
David Craib

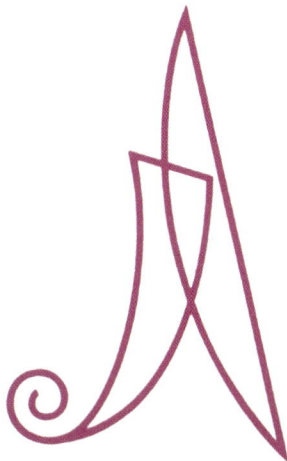

Client:
White Horse Cosmetics Co.
Nature of Business:
Cosmetics
Design Firm:
Kan & Lau Design Consultants
Art Directors:
Kan Tai-keung,
Freeman Lau Sui Hong
Designer:
Freeman Lau Sui Hong

Client:
Alta Beverage Bottle Packaging
Nature of Business:
Spring water bottling/distribution
Design Firm:
Hornall Anderson Design
Works, Inc.
Art Director:
Jack Anderson
Designers:
Jack Anderson,
Larry Anderson, Julie Keenan
Illustrator:
Dave Julian

Client:
Barcode
Nature of Business:
Beverage
Design Firm:
Supon Design Group
Art Director:
Supon Phornirulit
Designer:
Alexander Chang

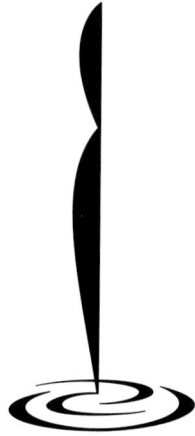

Client:
Chow Sang Sang Group
Nature of Business:
Jewelry retail
Design Firm:
Kan & Lau Design Consultants
Art Director:
Kan Tai-keung, Freeman Lau,
Clement Yick
Designers:
Clement Yick Tat Wa

Client:
Best Cellars
Nature of Business:
Wine retail/distribution
Design Firm:
Hornall Anderson Design Works, Inc.
Art Director:
Jack Anderson
Designers:
Jack Anderson, Lisa Cerveny,
Jana Wilson

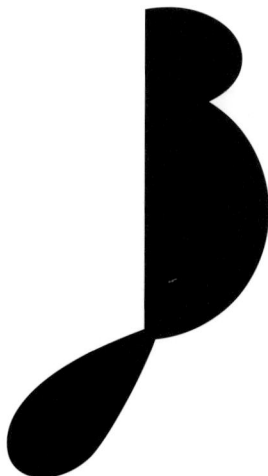

Client:
Beaver Construction
Design Firm:
DogStar
Art Director:
Terry Slaughter, Slaughter-Hanson
Designers:
Terry Slaughter, Rodney Davidson
Illustrator:
Rodney Davidson

Client:
Edi Berk
Nature of Business:
Design
Design Firm:
KROG
Art Director:
Edi Berk

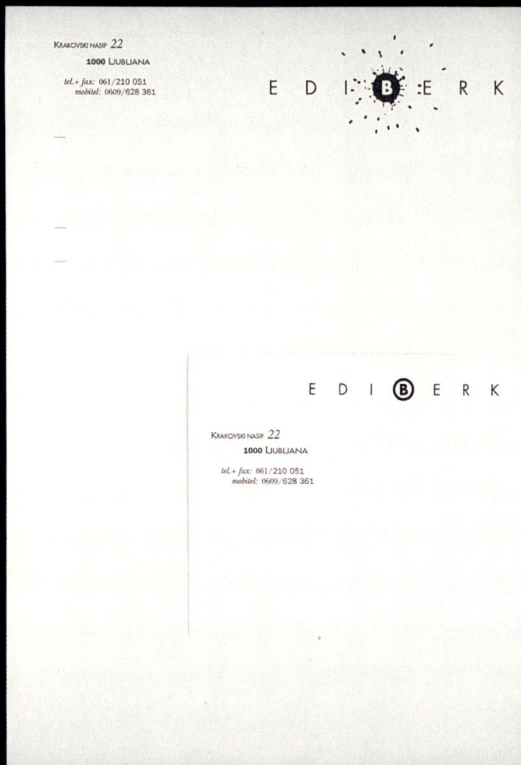

EDI **B** ERK

Krakovski nasp *22*
1000 LJUBLJANA
tel.+ fax: 061/210 051
mobitel: 0609/628 361

EDI **B** ERK

Krakovski nasp *22*
1000 LJUBLJANA
tel.+ fax: 061/210 051
mobitel: 0609/628 361

Client:
Best Cellars
Nature of Business:
Wine retail/distribution
Design Firm:
Hornall Anderson Design Works, Inc.
Art Director:
Jack Anderson
Designers:
Jack Anderson, Lisa Cerveny,
Jana Wilson

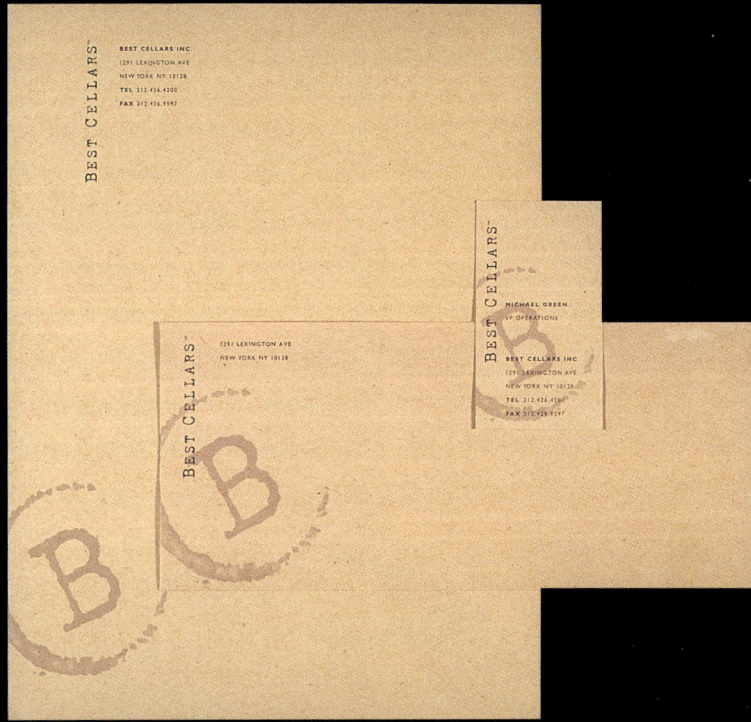

BEST CELLARS™

BEST CELLARS INC
1291 LEXINGTON AVE
NEW YORK NY 10128
TEL 212.426.4200
FAX 212.426.9597

BEST CELLARS™

MICHAEL GREEN
VP OPERATIONS

BEST CELLARS INC
1291 LEXINGTON AVE
NEW YORK NY 10128
TEL 212.426.4200
FAX 212.426.9597

BEST CELLARS™

1291 LEXINGTON AVE
NEW YORK NY 10128

BEST CELLARS™

Client:
Chimera Design
Nature of Business
Design
Design Firm:
Chimera Design
Designer:
John Magart

Client:
The Centris Group, Inc.
Nature of Business:
Reinsurance
Design Firm:
White Design, Inc.
Art Director:
Jamie Graupner
Designer:
David Matea
Illustrator:
David Matea
Copywriter:
Eric LeBrecque

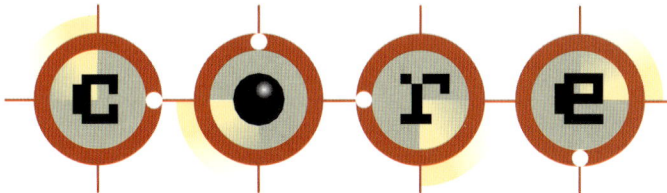

Client:
Core Digital Pictures
Nature of Business
Digital special effects and animation
Design Firm:
Overdrive Design
Art Directors:
James Wilson, Jay Wilson (animation)
Designer:
James Wilson
Illustrator:
James Wilson

Client:
Edinger
Nature of Business:
Carpentry
Design Firm:
Mag. Lothar Amilian Heinzle
Art Director:
Heinzle Lothar Amilian

Client:
Hard Boiled Egg
Nature of Business:
Software development
Design Firm:
Virus Design
Art Director:
Isabelle Lussier

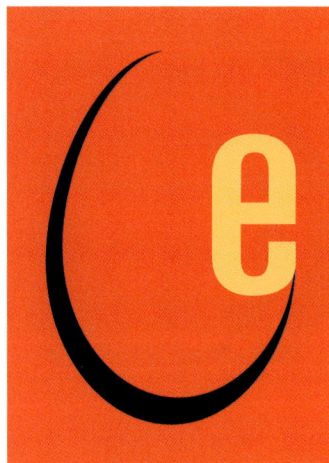

Client:
City of Evanston
Nature of Business:
Park and recreation
Design Firm:
Michael Stanard, Inc.
Art Director:
Michael Stanard
Designer:
Kristy Vandekerckhove
Illustrator:
Kristy Vandekerckhove

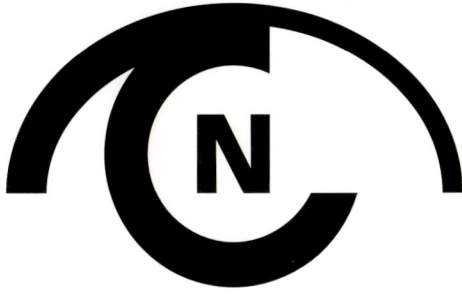

Client:
Con Nikolovski
Nature of Business:
Photography
Design Firm:
Marcus Lee Design Pty. Ltd.
Art Director:
Marcus Lee
Designer:
George Margaritis

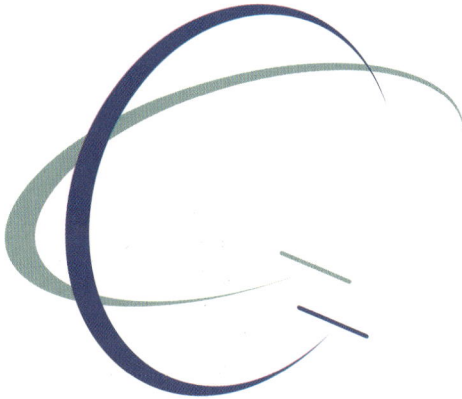

Client:
The Gauntlett Group
Nature of Business:
Environmental solutions
Design Firm:
Bruce Yelaska Design
Art Director:
Bruce Yelaska

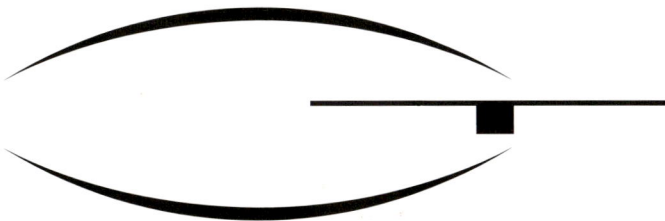

Client:
Grantek Systems Integration
Nature of Business:
Systems software for manufacturing
Design Firm:
The Riordan Design Group, Inc.
Art Director:
Ric Riordan
Designer:
Dan Wheaton

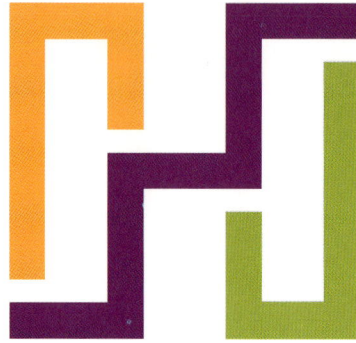

Client:
Health Steps
Nature of Business:
Medical consulting
Design Firm:
RBMM
Art Director:
Tom Nynas
Illustrator:
Tom Nynas

Client:
Italian Hotel Reservation Center
Nature of Business:
Travel reservation
Design Firm:
Julia Tam Design
Art Director:
Julia Chong Tam
Illustrator:
Julia Chong Tam

Client:
Hotel Association of Canada
Nature of Business:
Lobby group for hotel and
allied industries
Design Firm:
Ricochet Creative Thinking
Art Director:
Steve Zelle

proof

Client:
Wind River Visual Communications
Nature of Business:
Internet logos
Design Firm:
Wind River Visual Communications
Art Director:
David Coleman
Designer:
Jeanna Pool

Client:
Pomurski sejem
Nature of Business:
Packaging fair
Design Firm:
KROG
Art Director:
Edi Berk

Client:
Kiku Obata & Company
Nature of Business:
Environmental graphic design
Design Firm:
Kiku Obata & Company
Art Director:
Kiku Obata
Designer:
Rich Nelson

Client:
Lionel Corporation
Nature of Business:
Model railroad toys
Design Firm:
Michael Stanard, Inc.
Art Directors:
Michael Stanard, Marc Fuhrman
Designer:
Marc Fuhrman

Client:
Tom Stewart
Nature of Business:
Personal yacht logo
Design Firm:
Hornall Anderson Design Works, Inc.
Art Director:
Jack Anderson
Designers:
Jack Anderson, Nicole Bloss

Client:
Miracle Car Wash
Nature of Business:
Automated car wash
Design Firm:
Refinery Design Co.
Art Director:
Michael Schmalz

Client:
M Design Office
Nature of Business:
Design
Design Firm:
M Design Office

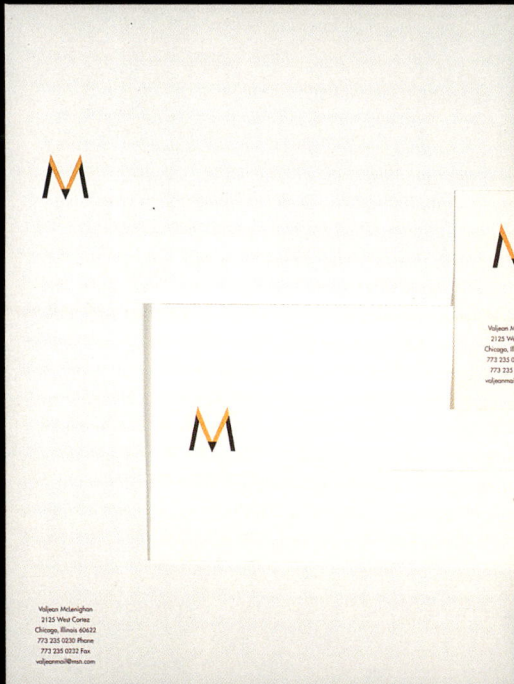

Client:
Valjean McLenighan
Nature of Business:
Corporate communications
Design Firm:
Kym Abrams Design
Art Director:
Kym Abrams
Designer:
Kerry LaCoste
Illustrator:
Kerry LaCoste

Client:
Smith Properties
Nature of Business:
Building maintenance
Design Firm:
Overdrive Design
Art Director:
James Wilson
Illustrator:
Dan Rempel

SMITH PROPERTY SERVICES

Client:
First Night Evanston
Nature of Business:
New Year's celebration
Design Firm:
Michael Stanard, Inc.
Art Director:
Michael Stanard
Designer:
Michael Chang

FIRST
NIGHT
EVANSTON

NOYES CULTURAL
ARTS CENTER
927 NOYES STREET
EVANSTON, ILLINOIS
60201-2799

Client:
Pacific Dental Care
Nature of Business:
Dentistry
Design Firm:
Sheehan Design
Art Director:
Jamie Sheehan

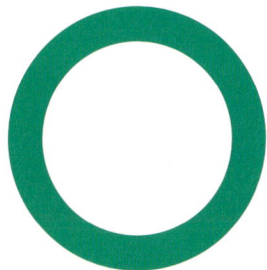

Client:
Quantum
Nature of Business:
Racing sail design/manufacture
Design Firm:
Supon Design Group
Art Director:
Supon Phornirunlit
Designer:
Andrew Berman

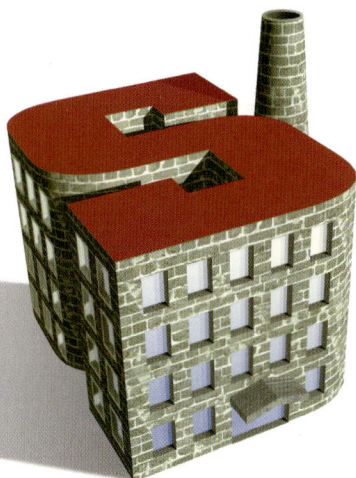

Client:
Smith Properties
Nature of Business:
Building maintenance
Design Firm:
Overdrive Design
Art Director:
James Wilson
Illustrator:
Dan Rempel

Client:
Andreas Karl Design
Nature of Business:
Design
Design Firm:
Andreas Karl Design
Art Director:
Andreas Karl

Client:
Sunfactors
Nature of Business:
Pharmaceutical products
Design Firm:
Kilmer & Kilmer
Art Director:
Richard Kilmer

Client:
Samuels, Yoelin, Kantor,
Seymour & Spinrad
Nature of Business:
Law firm
Design Firm:
Jeff Fisher Logo Motives
Art Director:
Jeff Fisher
Illustrator:
Jeff Fisher

Client:
Swieter Design U.S.
Nature of Business:
Multi-disciplinary communication
Design Firm:
Swieter Design U.S.
Art Directors:
John Swieter, Mark Ford
Designer:
Mark Ford

Client:
Supon Design Group
Nature of Business:
Design Studio
Design Firm:
Supon Design Group
Art Director:
Supon Phornirunlit
Designer:
Sharisse Steber

Client:
Linacre Urology
Design Firm:
Marcus Lee Design Pty. Ltd.
Art Director:
Marcus Lee
Designer:
George Margaritis

Client:
Vodododo, Ljubljana
Nature of Business:
Water supply
Design Firm:
KROG
Art Director:
Edi Berk

Client:
VIOSH Australia
Nature of Business:
Occupational safety and health
research
Design Firm:
Peter Lambert Design
Art Director:
Peter Lambert
Designers:
Peter Lambert, Paul McKenna

Client:
Wichita State University
Men's Crew Team
Design Firm:
Gardner Design
Art Director:
Brian Miller
Illustrator:
Brian Miller

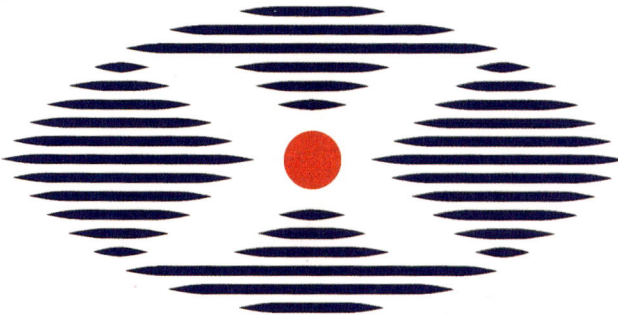

Client:
Media Concern
Nature of Business:
Pressure group
Design Firm:
Kan & Lau Design Consultants
Art Director:
Freeman Lau Siu Hong

Client:
Express Couriers
Design Firm:
Swieter Design U.S.
Art Director:
John Swieter
Designer:
Julie Poth

Client:
Interex
Nature of Business:
Computer product manufacture
Design Firm:
Insight Design Communications
Art Directors:
Sherrie and Tracy Holdeman
Illustrators:
Sherrie and Tracy Holdeman

Client:
AutoDesk
Nature of Business:
Drawing art
Design Firm:
Bruce Yelaska Design
Art Director:
John Seminerio
Designer:
Bruce Yelaska

Client:
X Century Studios
Design Firm:
Shimokochi/Reeves
Art Directors:
Mamoru Shimokochi, Anne Reeves
Designer:
Mamoru Shimokochi

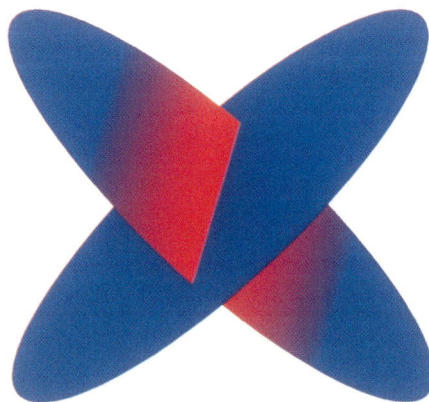

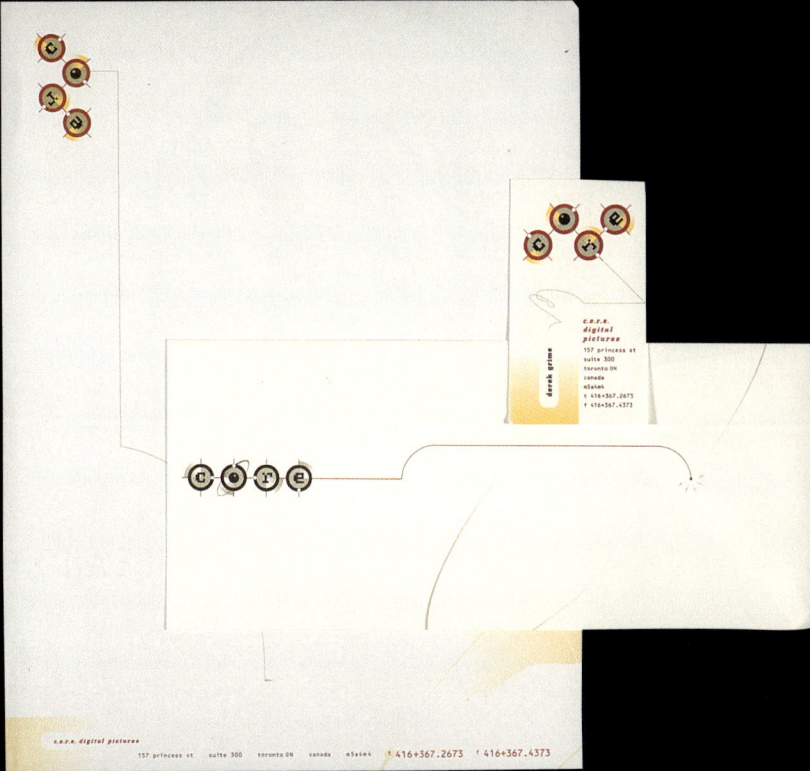

Client:
Core Digital Pictures
Nature of Business:
Digital special effects and animation
Design Firm:
Overdrive Design
Art Directors:
James Wilson, Jan Wilson
Designer:
James Wilson

c.o.r.e.
digital
pictures
157 princess st
suite 300
toronto ON
canada
m5a4m4
t 416+367.2673
f 416+367.4373

derek grime

c o r e

c.o.r.e. digital pictures

157 princess st.   suite 300   toronto ON   canada   m5a4m4   t 416+367.2673   f 416+367.4373

Client:
Fine Design Group
Nature of Business:
Graphic design
Design Firm:
Fine Design Group
Art Director:
Kenn Fine
Designer:
Lydia Ricci

fine design group

1875 Lombard Street San Francisco, CA 94123 415.922.2100 /922.2191

1875 Lombard St.
San Francisco
CA 94123
415.922.2100
/922.2191
yes@finedesign.com

Yvette Fine

fine design group
1875 Lombard Street San Francisco, CA 94123

Client:
Hideaki Miyake
Nature of Business:
Photography
Design Firm:
Kirima Design Office
Art Director:
Harumi Kirima

Client:
Canadian Technology
Human Resources Board
Nature of Business:
Promotion of technology education
Design Firm:
Ricochet Creative Thinking
Art Director:
Steve Zelle

Client:
Tech Knowledge
Nature of Business:
Web site design
Design Firm:
Born to Design
Art Director:
Todd Adkins

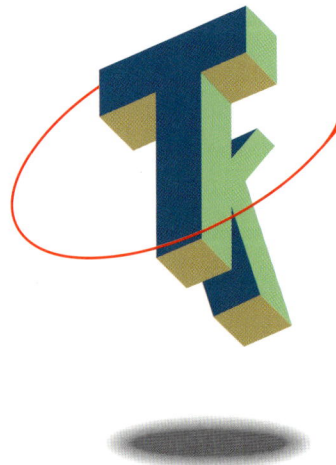

Client:
Kelly Pierce
Nature of Business:
Art
Design Firm:
Swieter Design U.S.
Art Director:
Mark Ford

Client:
Moda
Nature of Business:
Modern home furnishings
Design Firm:
Zust & Company
Art Director:
Mark Zust

Client:
Department of Power
Nature of Business:
Power cycling spin studio
Design Firm:
Simple Green In-House Design
Art Director:
Mike Brower
Designers:
Russell Acol, Mike Brower

Client:
Mortensen Design
Nature of Business:
Design
Design Firm:
Mortensen Design
Art Directors:
Gordon Mortensen
Designers:
Gordon Mortensen, Diana L.
Kauzlarich

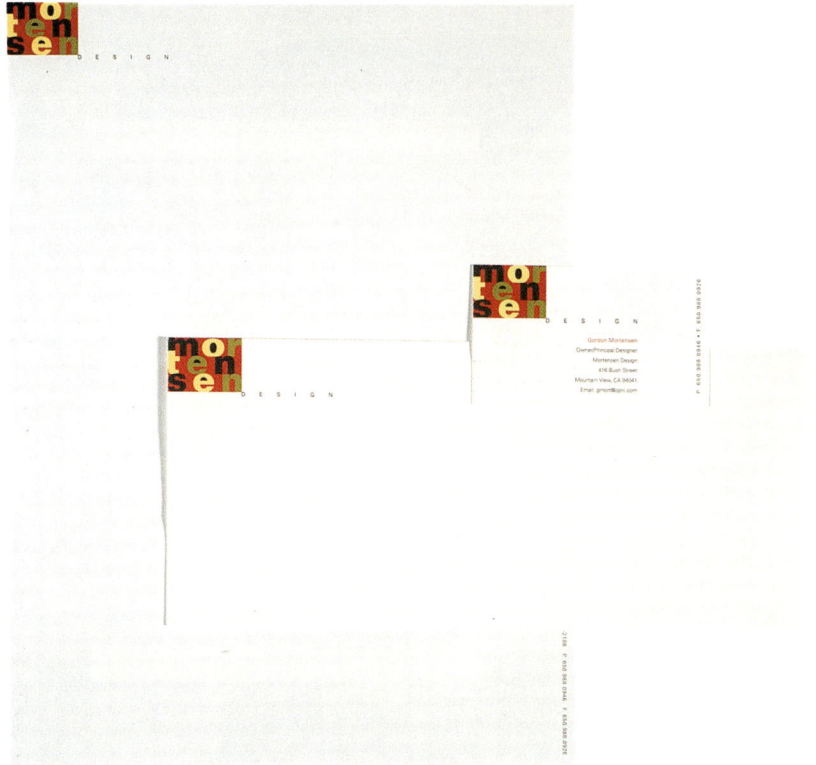

Client:
National Gallery Society of Victoria
Nature of Business:
Art
Design Firm:
Mammoliti Chan Design
Art Director:
Tony Mammoliti
Designer:
Chwee Kuan Chan
Illustrator:
Chwee Kuan Chan

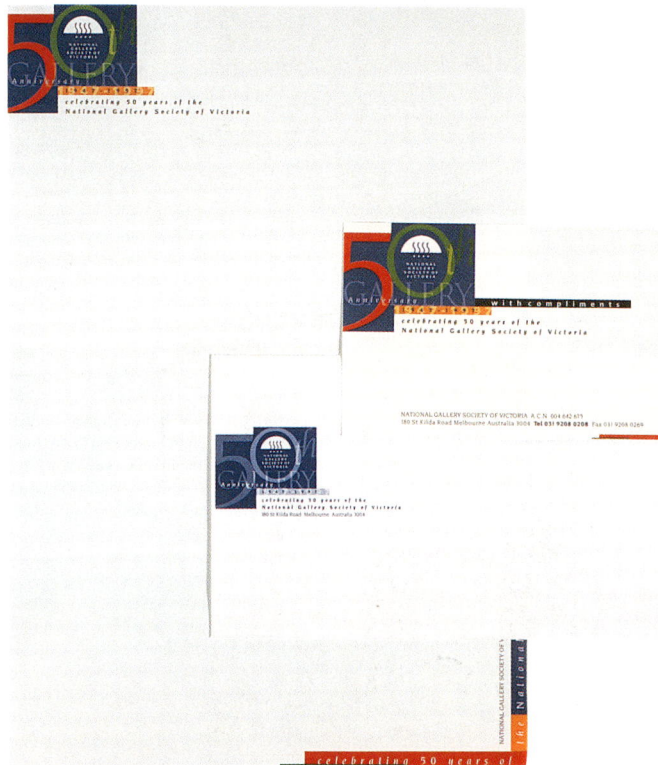

Client:
Ministry of Education and Sport
Nature of Business:
Education
Design Firm:
Bons d.o.o.
Art Director:
Zarja Vintar

Client:
USDA
Nature of Business:
Government Agency
Design Firm:
Supon Design Group
Art Director:
Supon Phornmirunlit
Designer:
Andy Dolan

Client:
Grider and Company
Nature of Business:
Accounting
Design Firm:
Gardner Design
Art Director:
Bill Gardner

Client:
Tops Restaurants
Nature of Business:
Fast food
Design Firm:
Zamboo
Art Directors:
Dave Zambotti, Becca Bootes

TOPS

Client:
Colts Drum and Bugle Corporation
Nature of Business:
Marching band
Design Firm:
McCullough Creative Group
Art Director:
Michael Schmalz

Client:
Jill, Chris, Martha & Claudia
Nature of Business:
AIDS bike ride
Design Firm:
Bruce E. Morgan Graphic Design
Art Director:
Bruce E. Morgan

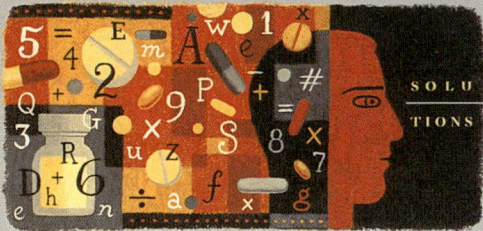

Client:
Migliara/Kaplan Associates
Nature of Business:
Health care market resear
Design Firm:
Gibson Creative
Art Director:
Bob Kiernan
Illustrator:
James Steinberg

SOLU
TIONS

MIGLIARA / KAPLAN ASSOCIATES

perspective | INNOVATION | DIRECTION

Inventive. Unique. Ingenious. Migliara/Kaplan takes even the standard ways of gathering research and creates something new every single time. Why? Because we know that every single question requires a different answer. That no two issues are ever the same. A good product strategy demands a highly customized, bold approach to healthcare marketing research.

Migliara/Kaplan was the first in our industry to apply this philosophy, and the results have been predictably and consistently successful. By applying new methodologies to standard research techniques, we are able to define an approach that best fits your particular issue. And to find the answers that best fit your questions.

But we haven't just put a new spin on the standard approaches. We are continually creating completely new methodologies. In fact, some of our methods are exclusive and proprietary. One of the most revolutionary of these is the Migliara/Kaplan Triad.

The Migliara/Kaplan Triad is just one example of how innovative thinking can change a brand's probability of success. The Triad is a revolutionary approach that has literally changed the way healthcare marketing research is gathered, analyzed, and understood. From within our deep well of industry resources and practical experience, the Triad takes shape. An approach that looks at all three sides of the healthcare industry—the physician, the payer, and the patient—as well as the relationships between them.

The Migliara/Kaplan Triad gives you a real competitive advantage. You can enter the field earlier, forecast sales more accurately, launch your product sooner, reduce your risks, and anticipate roadblocks. You can even cut down on research and development time.

The ability to blaze new trails. The imagination to shake things up. The expertise to rearrange the world of healthcare research and put it back together in a whole new way. It's about getting innova-tive answers to all the questions you have. And to some you may never have thought to ask.

What is the most viable promotional strategy to leverage the benefits of my brand?

How likely is managed care to put my product on their formulary?

HOW DOES **innovation** LEAD TO ANSWERS?

By asking the questions that have already been asked in A WHOLE NEW WAY. And some that you may never have thought to ask.

INNOVATION

Client:
Liberty Yogourt
Nature of Business:
Foods manufacturer
Design Firm:
Tarzan Communications, Inc.
Art Directors:
George Fok, Daniel Fortin

Svelte

Client:
Gra
Nature of Business:
Accessories
Design Firm:
Interface Designers
Art Director:
Isabel Augusta
Illustrator (typography):
Isabel Augusta

GRA

ACESSÓRIOS & CO.

Client:
Lenny
Nature of Business:
Swimwear
Design Firm:
Interface Designers
Art Director:
Gustavo Portela
Illustrator (typography):
Gustavo Portela

Lenny

Client:
Talking Rain Corporation
Nature of Business:
Bottled water distribution
Design Firm:
Hornall Anderson Design Works, Inc.
Art Director:
Jack Anderson
Designers:
Jack Anderson, Jana Nishi
Illustrator:
Julia LaPine

Client:
Grand Palace Foods
Nature of Business:
Bottled water distribution
Design Firm:
Supon Design Group
Art Director:
Supon Phornirunlit
Designer:
Tom Klinedinst
Illustrator:
Tom Klinedinst

Client:
David Scott
Photography
Design Firm:
Viva Dolan Communications and
Design
Art Director:
Frank Viva
Designer:
Julie Opatousky

Client:
Andy Wong/Studio Point
Nature of Business:
Photography
Design Firm:
Genesis Advertising Co.
Art Director:
James Wai Mo Leung
Illustrator:
James Wai Mo Leung

media **sage**
incorporated

3044 Bloor Street West
Suite 223
Toronto, Ontario
M8X 1C4

Executive Training

Public Relations
Consulting

Speechwriting

3044 Bloor Street West
Suite 223
Toronto, Ontario
M8X 1C4

media **sage**
incorporated

3044 Bloor Street West
Suite 223
Toronto, Ontario
M8X 1C4

media **sage**
incorporated

Marianne Gobeil
President

tel: 416 231 6877
fax: 416 231 5878
mediasage@netcom.ca

tel: 416 231 6877
fax: 416 231 5878
mediasage@netcom.ca

Client:
Media Sage Inc.
Nature of Business:
Public relations consulting
Design Firm:
Q30 Design
Art Director:
Peter Scott

MANAGEMENT **matters**
incorporated

tel. 416 231 0722   3044 Bloor Street West
fax. 416 231 5878   Suite 223
mgmtmtrs@compuserve.com   Toronto, Ontario
M8X 1C4

MANAGEMENT **matters**
incorporated

Morley Kerr

tel. 416 231 0722   3044 Bloor Street West
fax. 416 231 5878   Suite 223
mgmtmtrs@compuserve.com   Toronto, Ontario
M8X 1C4

MANAGEMENT **matters**
incorporated

3044 Bloor Street West
Suite 223
Toronto, Ontario
M8X 1C4

Client:
Management Matters
Nature of Business:
Management consulting
Design Firm:
Q30 Design
Art Director:
Peter Scott
Designer:
Nadine Chassé

Client:
Pulsar Internacional
Nature of Business:
Multi-level marketing
Design Firm:
Signi
Art Director:
Daniel Castelao

ORBIS

Client:
Brown Printing
Design Firm:
Larsen Design + Interactive
Art Director:
Richelle Huff
Designer:
Sascha Boecker

BROWN

Client:
McCaw
Nature of Business:
Wireless communications
Design Firm:
Hornall Anderson Design Works, Inc.
Art Director:
Jack Anderson
Designers:
Jack Anderson, Suzanne Haddon,
David Bates, Mary Hermes, Heidi
Favour, Mary Chin Hutchison,
Virginia Le

McCAW

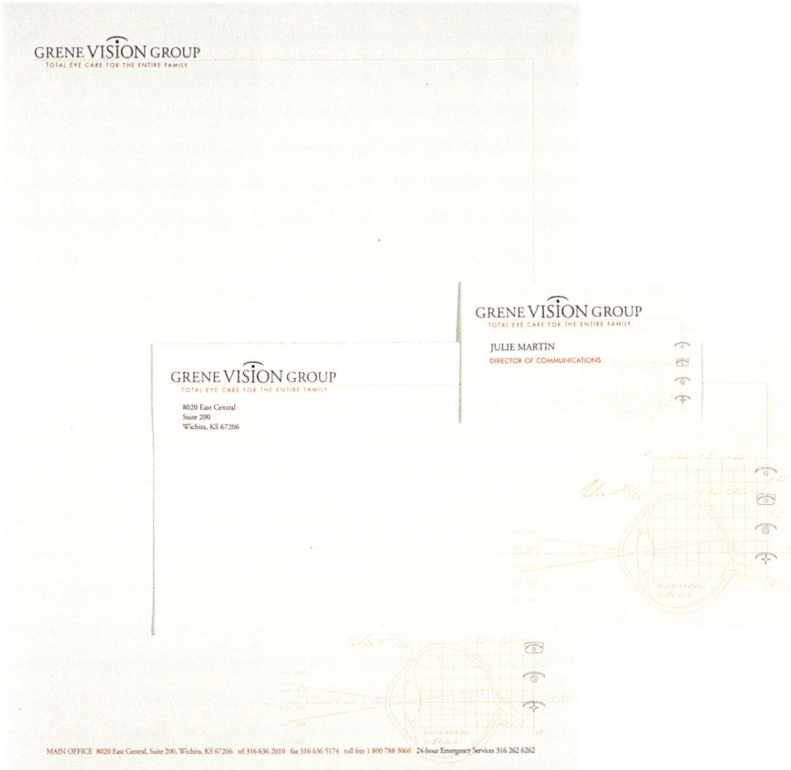

Client:
Grene Vision Group
Nature of Business:
Eye care
Design Firm:
Insight Design Communications
Art Director:
Sherrie and Tracy Holdeman
Illustrator:
Sherrie and Tracy Holdeman

Client:
Rock Island Studios
Nature of Business:
Photography
Design Firm:
Insight Design Communications
Art Director:
Sherrie and Tracy Holdeman
Illustrator:
Sherrie and Tracy Holdeman

Client:
Visual Marketing Associates
Nature of Business:
Design
Design Firm:
Visual Marketing Associates
Art Director:
Lynn Sampson

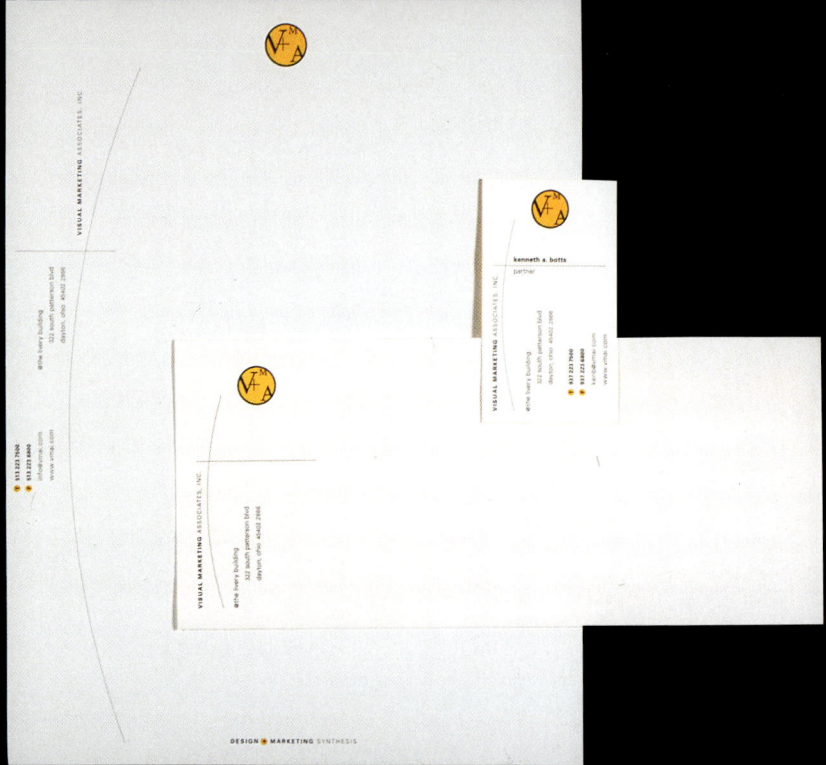

Client:
Fleming Design Group
Nature of Business:
Graphic design
Design Firm:
Fleming Design Group
Art Director:
Blair Pocock
Designer:
Marcus Braun

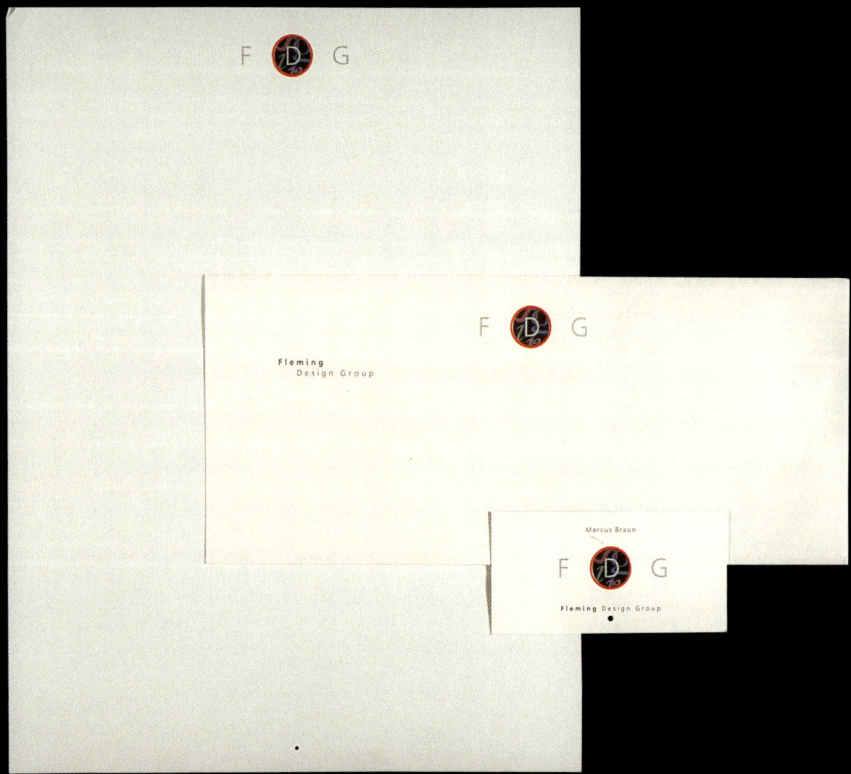

cloud

Client:
Cloud Nine
Nature of Business:
Confectionery
Design Firm:
Hornall Anderson Design Works, Inc.
Art Director:
Jack Anderson
Designers:
Jack Anderson, Jana Nishi, David
Bates, Sonja Max

Stillwaters™

Client:
Total Quality Apparel
Nature of Business:
Outdoor clothing
Design Firm:
Simple Green
Art Director:
Mike Brower
Illustrator:
Mike Brower

Scubalogy

Basic, Advanced & Specialty SCUBA Instruction

Client:
Scubalogy, Inc.
Nature of Business:
SCUBA diving instruction
Design Firm:
Christopher Gorz Design
Art Director:
Chris Gorz

Client:
NetStar Communications Inc.
Nature of Business:
Television and broadcast services
Design Firm:
Tudhope Associates Inc.
Art Director:
Ian C. Tudhope
Designer:
Michael Stokley

Client:
Extreme Audio
Nature of Business:
Car audio installation
Design Firm:
Simantel Group
Art Director:
Becky Krohe

Client:
Franklin Realty Advisors
Nature of Business:
Real Estate
Design Firm:
Sasoki Associates, Inc.
Art Director:
M.B. Sawyer
Designers:
M.B. Sawyer, Susan Hoy

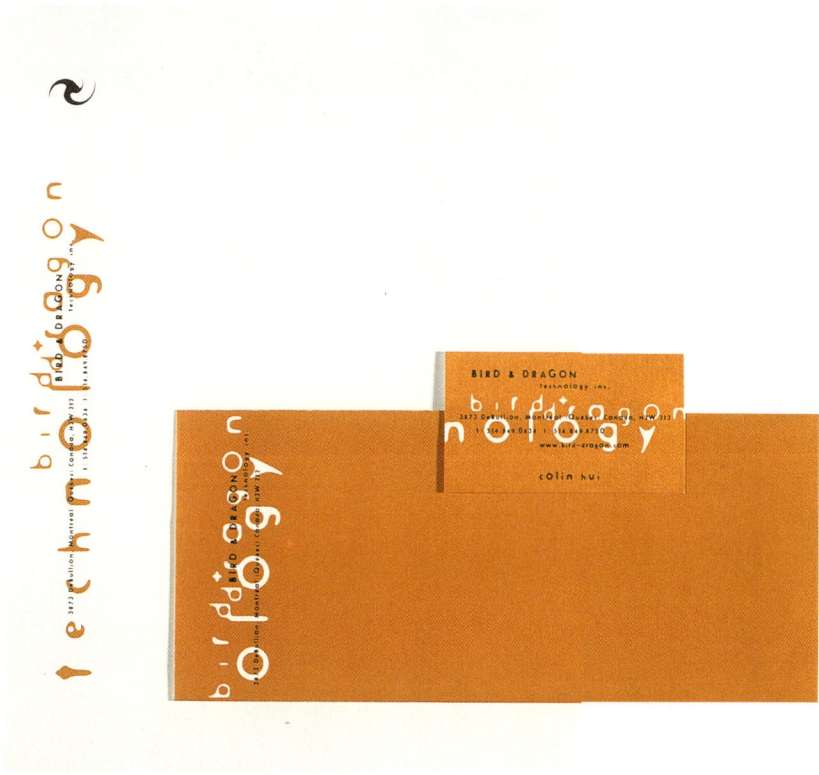

Client:
Bird and Dragon Technologies
Nature of Business:
Software development
Design Firm:
Tarzan Communications, Inc.
Art Directors:
Daniel Fortin, Gorge Fok
Designer:
Bob Beck

Client:
Fuszion Art + Design
Nature of Business:
Graphic design
Design Firm:
Fuszion Art + Design
Art Director:
Richard Lee Heffner
Designers:
Richard Heffner, Tony Fletcher,
Mike Pfister

Client:
DataCard
Nature of Business:
Manufacturing
Design Firm:
Larsen Design + Interactive
Art Directors:
Tim Larsen, Nancy Whittlesey
Designer:
David Schultz
Illustrator:
David Schultz

jigsaw™

Client:
The Minacs Group Inc.
Nature of Business:
Telefficiency services
Design Firm:
The Riordan Design Group Inc.
Art Director:
Ric Riordan
Designer:
Dan Wheaton

(minacs)

Client:
Canuck Office Furnishings
Design Firm:
Image Design Communications Inc.
Art Director:
Phil Otto

canuck

Client:
Interactive Group
Nature of Business:
ERP Software
Design Firm:
Vaughn/Wedeen Creative
Art Director:
Steve Wedeen

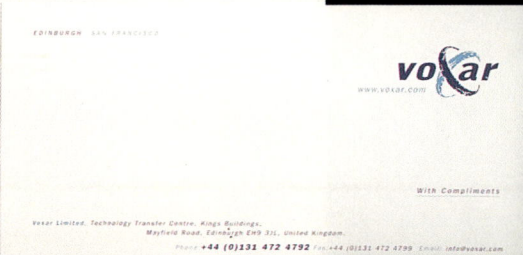

Client:
Voxar Ltd.
Nature of Business:
Medical 3D visualization software
Design Firm:
Graphic Partners
Designer:
Jack Rodgers

Client:
CSI Digital
Nature of Business:
Computer equipment retail
Design Firm:
Hornall Anderson Design Works, Inc.
Art Director:
John Hornall
Designers:
David Bates, Margaret Long,
John Anicker

You can't afford to have equipment down. After all, "uptime" means profitability. CSI Digital understands this, and we have designed our technical support services around this concept.

HEVER BEFORE HAS TECHNOLOGY BEEN SO CLOSELY TIED TO THE SUCCESS OF YOUR BUSINESS

XCEL

Client:
Xcel
Nature of Business:
Athletic beverage distribution
Design Firm:
Hornall Anderson Design Works, Inc.
Art Director:
Jack Anderson
Designers:
Jack Anderson, Larry Anderson,
Julie Keenan

NOVASTAR

Client:
NovaStar Real Estate, Inc.
Design Firm:
Steve Trapero Design
Art Director:
Steve Trapero

A + R

Client:
A+R Medical Supply
Nature of Business:
Medical supply distribution
Design Firm:
Vaughn/Wedeen Creative
Art Director:
Steve Wedeen

Client:
MGM
Nature of Business:
Film
Design Firm:
Mike Salisbury Communications
Art Director:
Mike Salisbury
Illustrator:
Pat Linse

Client:
Big Weenie Records
Nature of Business:
Alternative record label
Design Firm:
Tracy Sabin Graphic Design
Art Director:
Eero Sabin
Designer:
Tracy Sabin
Illustrator:
Tracy Sabin

Client:
Aviva Communications
Nature of Business:
Video and film production
Design Firm:
Tarzan Communications Inc.
Art Directors:
Daniel Fortin, George Fok
Designer:
Michel Valois

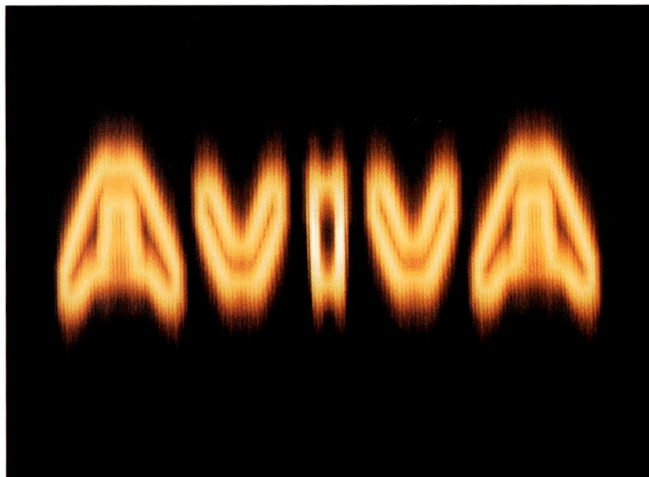

400 n. 5th street, suite 1050, phoenix, az 85004
info@enx.com http://www.enx.com

x
e—n—x

david francis
consultant

400 n. 5th street, suite 1050
phoenix, az 85004

info@enx.com
http://www.enx.com

x
e—n—x

fax: 602.257.4457
voice: 602.257.7800

voice: 602.257.7800   fax: 602.257.4457

Client:
Enx
Nature of Business:
Energy exchange brokerage services
Design Firm:
After Hours Creative
Art Director:
After Hours Creative

foundation

1715 east olive way

top floor

seattle, wa 98102-5614

phone 206 860 8800

fax 206 860 8809

foundation
1715 east olive way
top floor
seattle, wa 98102-5614
phone 206 860 8800
fax 206 860 8809

giorgio davanzo
design manager

foundation
1715 east olive way
top floor
seattle, wa 98102-5614

Client:
Foundation
Nature of Business:
Design
Design Firm:
Foundation
Art Director:
Lanny French
Designer:
Giorgio Davanzo

Client:
The Paper House Group
Nature of Business:
Paper sales
Design Firm:
Cozzolino Ellett Design D'Vision
Art Director:
Darren Ledwich
Illustrator:
Darren Ledwich

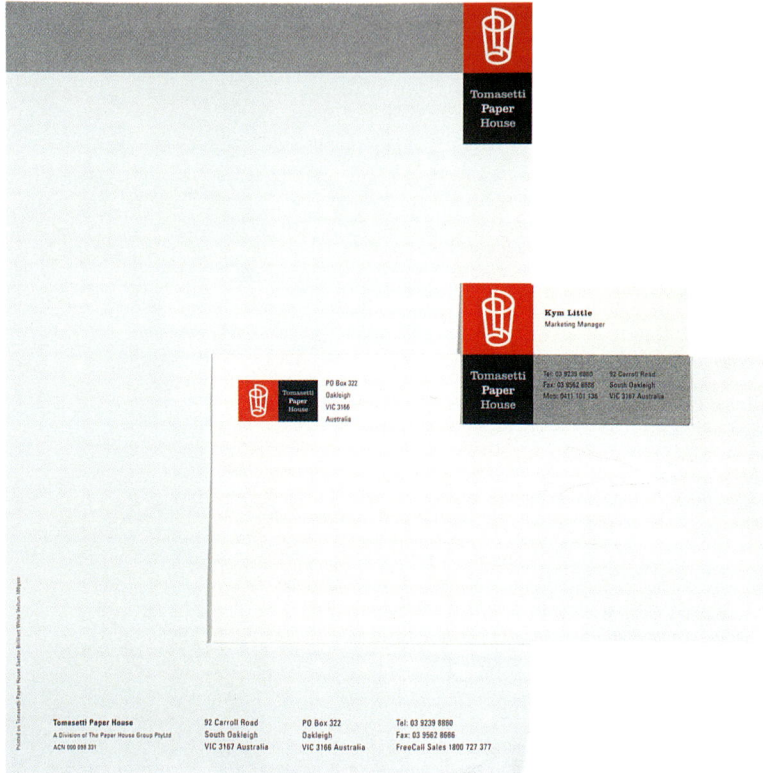

Client:
Pettit Integrated Inc.
Nature of Business:
Marketing and consulting
Design Firm:
The Riordan Design Group Inc.
Art Director:
Ric Riordan
Designer:
Dan Wheaton

FunWorks

Client:
Johnson & Johnson
Nature of Business:
Healthcare products
Design Firm:
Toni Schowalter Design
Art Director:
Toni Schowalter

gibson creative

Client:
Gibson Creative
Nature of Business:
Design and communications
Design Firm:
Gibson Creative
Art Director:
Bob Kiernan
Designers:
Bob Kiernan, Jenn Miller, Kirby Jones,
Mark Hausler, Juliette Brown

3BALDMEN PRODUCTIONS

Client:
3 Baldmen
Nature of Business:
Custom home furnishings
Design Firm:
Intersection Design
Art Director:
Jason Alger
Designer:
Daniel Bean

Client:
Starbucks Coffee Company
Nature of Business:
Coffee and specialty product retail
Design Firm:
Hornall Anderson Design Works, Inc.
Art Director:
Jack Anderson
Designers:
Jack Anderson, Julie Lock, Jana Nishi,
Julie Keenan, Mary Chin Hutchison

frappuccino ™

Client:
Makoto Ishihara
Nature of Business:
Entertainment planning and editing
Design Firm:
Kirima Design Office
Art Director:
Harumi Kirima

pop out of the box!
nude

Client:
Grupo Alfa
Nature of Business:
Telecommunications
Design Firm:
Signi
Designer:
Daniel Castelao

ONEXA

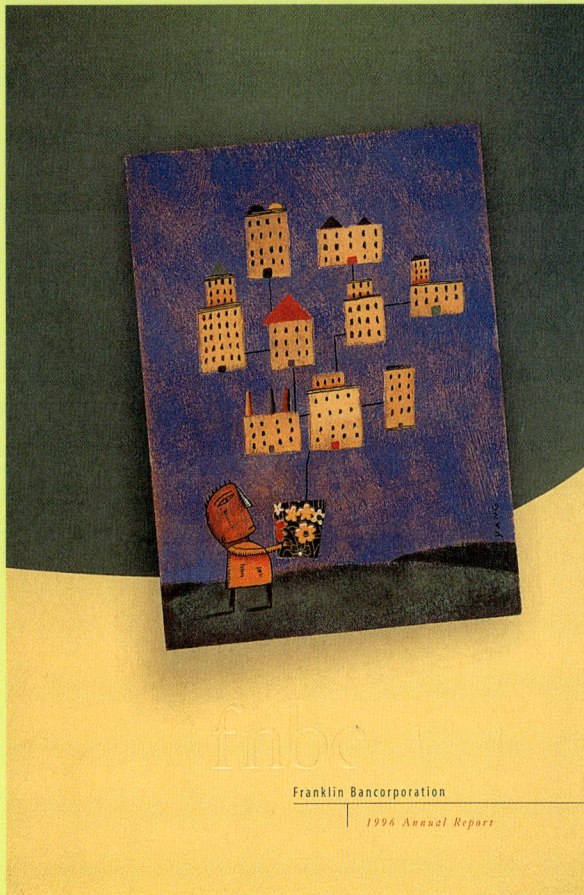

Client:
Franklin National Bank
Design Firm:
Gibson Creative
Art Director:
Juliette Brown
Illustrator:
James Yang

Franklin Bancorporation

1996 Annual Report

while significantly increasing both net and non-interest income, accounts for the stability of Franklin's productivity ratio which has improved from 67% in 1994 to 63% in both 1995 and 1996.

Employee related costs, occupancy and other overhead expenses totaled $12.7 million for 1996, as compared to $9.9 million for 1995. The largest component of non-interest expense, compensation and employee benefits, grew by $1.6 million, or 33%, from $4.9 million in 1995 to $6.5 million in 1996 as Franklin provided for qualified, experienced personnel necessary to continue to provide operational support to the Bank's growing customer base as well as staff our new locations. This increase in compensation expense accounted for 57% of the 1996 increase in non-interest expense.

Franklin's occupancy and furniture and equipment expense increased by $668 thousand, or 35%, from $1.9 million in 1995 to $2.6 million in 1996. This increase is due to the branch expansion as well as the technology improvements made to properly manage Franklin's transaction volume growth and provide new products and services.

The increase in all other non-interest expense for 1996 was $530 thousand, or 17%, from $3.1 million in 1995 to $3.6 million in 1996. That increase is primarily due to the technology and data processing improvements initiated in 1995 and expanded in 1996 as well as Franklin's increased commitment as sponsor of the Franklin National Bank Classic.

Non-interest expense increased 28% to $9.9 million in 1995 from $7.7 million in 1994. Compensation and employee benefits increased $1.1 million, or 28%, to $4.9 million in 1995 from $3.8 million in 1994. This increase was the result of doubling Franklin's D.C. branch network and merging with GWBC during 1995. This increase in compensation expense accounted for 50% of 1995's increase in non-interest expense. Franklin's occupancy and furniture and equipment expense increased $601 thousand, or 46%, from $1.3 million in 1994 to $1.9 million in 1995. That increase was also due to the branch expansion, the merger and the conversion to a new data processing system. The increase in other non-interest expense for 1995 was $511 thousand, or 20%, from $2.6 million in 1994 to $3.1 million in 1995. That increase was primarily due to the addition of Franklin-Virginia on April 1, 1995, whose 1995 non-interest expense was $440 thousand.

Franklin's provision for income taxes includes both federal and local income taxes. The increase in income tax expense to $2.9 million for 1996, from $2.3 million in 1995 and $1.1 million in 1994 is attributable to the significant increase in Franklin's net income and the annual limitations placed on the utilization

of Franklin's available tax loss carryforwards. Franklin's effective tax rate for 1996 was 39% compared to 41% for 1995. A reconciliation of the effective tax rate to the 1996 federal statutory rate of 34% can be found in Note 10 of the consolidated financial statements.

Franklin Bancorporation

22 *1996 Annual Report*

Client:
Via
Nature of Business:
Interior design
Design Firm:
Square One Design
Art Director:
Lin Ver Meulen
Designer:
Lisa Vitalbo
Illustrator:
Lisa Vitalbo
Printer:
D&D Printing Co.
Copywriter:
Judy Been

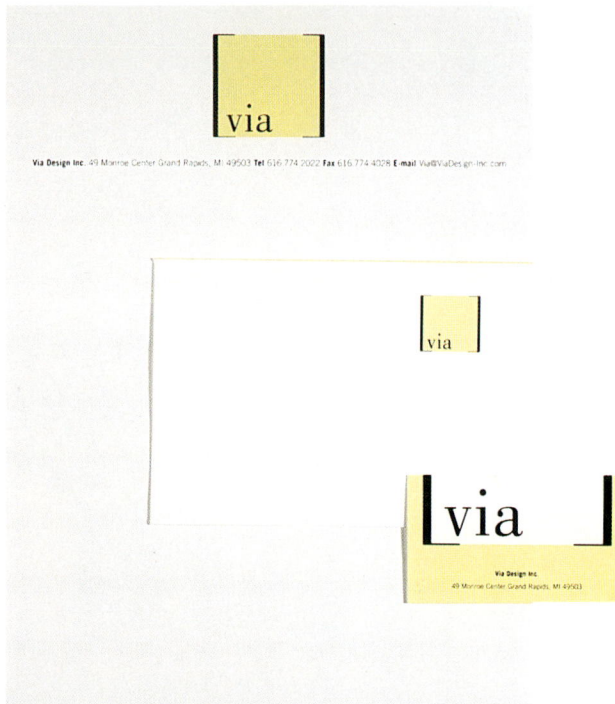

Client:
The Jones Design GmbH
Nature of Business:
Design
Design Firm:
The Jones Design GmbH
Art Directors:
André Baxmann, Ralf Huss
Designer:
Ralf Huss

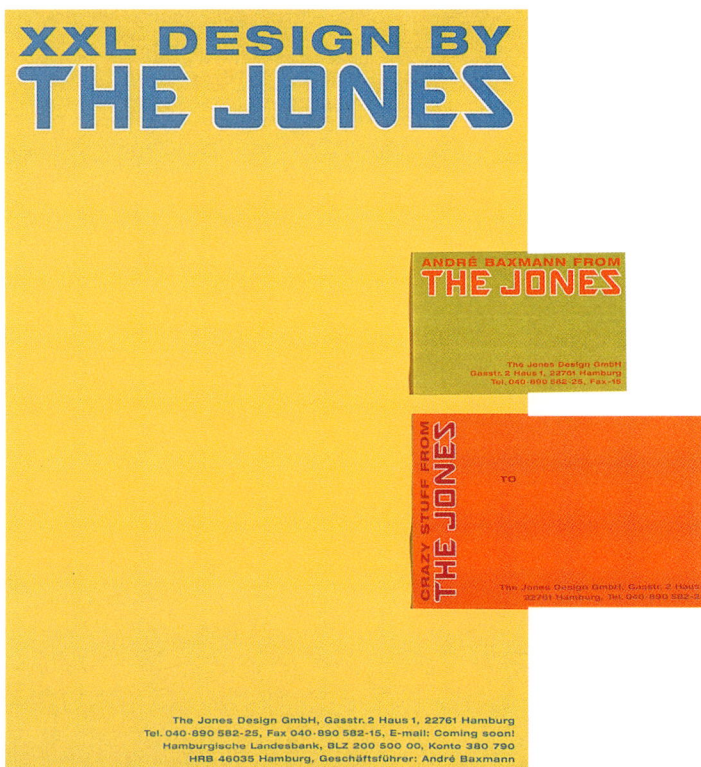

Client:
Cloudscape, Inc.
Nature of Business:
Java software
Design Firm:
Abrams Design Group
Art Director:
Colleen Abrams
Designers:
Sander Leech, Zeina Lama
Illustrator:
Sander Leech

Client:
COTCO Holdings Ltd.
Design Firm:
Kan & Lau Design Consultants
Art Director:
Freeman Lau Siu Hong
Designer:
Lam Wai Hung

Client:
Surfpolitix Europe
Nature of Business:
Ski manufacture
Design Firm:
Tarzan Communications Inc.
Art Directors:
Daniel Fortin, George Fok
Designers:
Marc Serre, Michel Valois

Client:
Constellar Corporation
Nature of Business:
Integrated hub software
Design Firm:
Abrams Design Group
Art Director:
Colleen Abrams
Designer:
Sandor Leech
Illustrator:
Sandor Leech

CONSTELLAR

Client:
InterSolv
Nature of Business:
Computer software development
Design Firm:
Steve Trapero Design
Art Director:
Deborah Howard
Designer:
Steve Trapero

InterLink

Client:
ASHP
Nature of Business:
Pharmacist association
Design Firm:
HC Design
Art Director:
Chuck Sundin
Designer:
Maria Sese Paul

MedAxon™

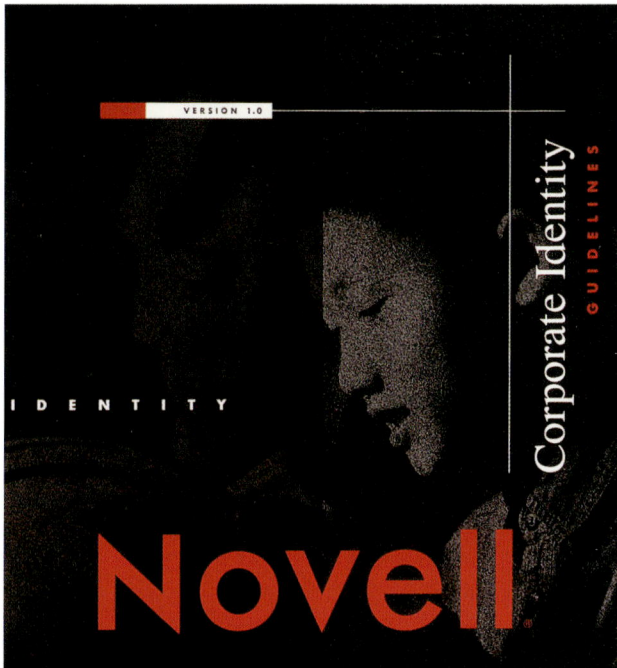

Client:
Novell, Inc.
Nature of Business:
Software manufacture
Design Firm:
Hornall Anderson Design Works, Inc.
Art Director:
Jack Anderson
Designers:
Jack Anderson, Bruce Branson-Meyer,
Larry Anderson

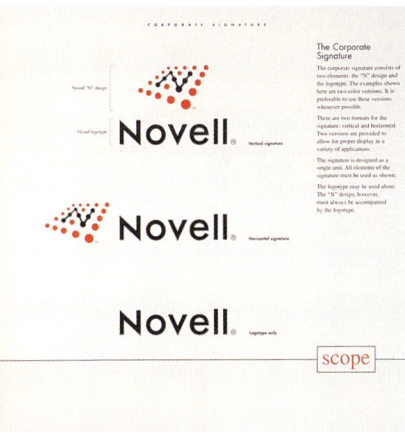

Client:
Icicle Seafoods, Inc.
Nature of Business:
Seafood processing
Design Firm:
Faine/Oller Productions, Inc.
Art Director:
Catherine Oller
Illustrator:
Martin French
Calligrapher:
Nancy Stentz

ICICLE®

Client:
H. Beale
Nature of Business:
Production company
Design Firm:
BRD Design
Art Director:
Peter King Robbins
Designer:
Sven Igawa

H. BEALE
COMPANY

Client:
E. B. Eddy
Nature of Business:
Recycled pulp manufacture
Design Firm:
Ricochet Creative Thinking
Art Director:
Steve Zelle

Blue Water
FIBER

Client:
Jamba Juice
Nature of Business:
Fresh juice
Design Firm:
Hornall Anderson Design Works, Inc.
Art Director:
Jack Anderson
Designers:
Jack Anderson, Lisa Cerveny, Suzanne Haddon
Illustrator:
Mits Katayama

Client:
Sensi
Nature of Business:
Footwear
Design Firm:
Foundation
Art Director:
Lanny French
Designer:
Jeff Larson

Client:
City of Port Phillip (Victoria, Australia)
Nature of Business:
Local community council
Design Firm:
Meg Robertson Design
Designer:
John Magart

Client:
Sweet Factory
Nature of Business:
Confectionery
Design Firm:
Michael Stanard, Inc.
Art Director:
Michael Stanard
Designer:
Kristy Vandekerckhove
Illustrator:
Kristy Vandekerckhove

Client:
Perfectly Round Productions
Nature of Business:
Creative TV production
Design Firm:
Insight Design Communications
Art Directors:
Sherrie and Tracy Holdeman
Illustrators:
Sherrie and Tracy Holdeman

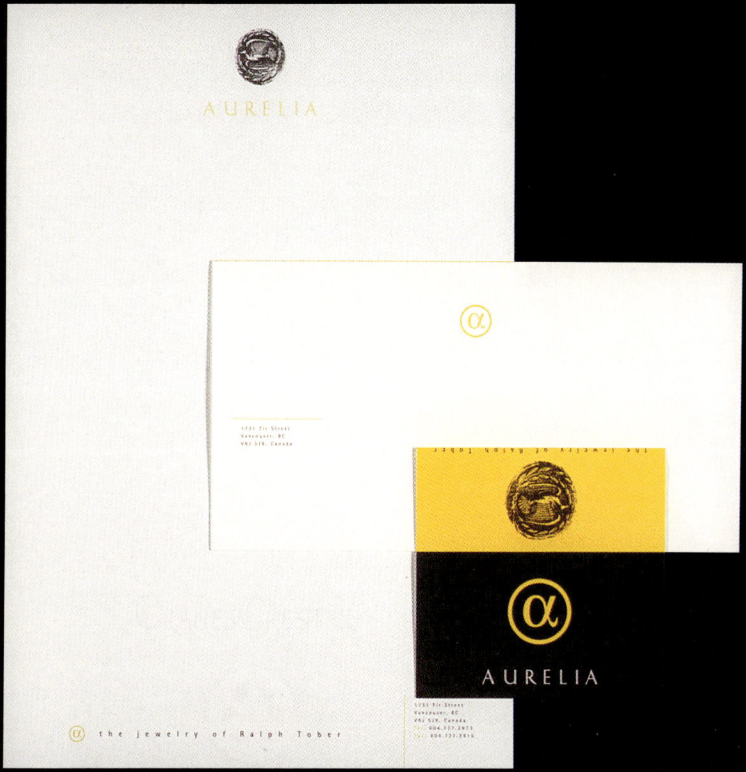

Client:
Aurelia
Nature of Business:
Goldsmith
Design Firm:
Bau Wow Design Group
Art Director:
Daniela Wood
Printer:
Classic Printing

Client:
deFine Design
Nature of Business:
Design
Design Firm:
deFine Design
Art Director:
Paul Minigiello

Client:
Souris & Petitti
Nature of Business:
Advertising
Design Firm:
Parable Communications Corp.
Creative Director:
Yannis Souris
Art Director:
David Craib
Illustrator:
Michael Custode

Client:
Golfoto
Nature of Business:
Golf course photography
Design Firm:
Greteman Group
Art Directors:
Sonia Greteman, James Strange
Illustrator:
James Strange

Client:
Signature Brands Ltd.
Design Firm:
Viva Dolan Communications +
Design
Art Director:
Frank Viva
Designer:
James Ryce
Illustrator:
Bill Russell

Souris & Petitti

SOURIS & PETITTI ADVERTISING/COMMUNICATIONS
53 BAYSWATER AVENUE, OTTAWA, CANADA. K1Y 2E7
TEL: (613) 722-7639 FAX: (613) 722-0049

Client:
Souris & Petitti
Nature of Business:
Advertising
Design Firm:
Parable Communications Cor
Creative Director:
Yannis Souris
Art Director:
David Craib
Illustrator:
Michael Custode
Printer:
M.O.M. Printing

kirurška poliklinika dr.lastrić

ordinacija za
proktologiju
flebologiju i
malu estetsku kirurgiju

kirurška poliklinika dr.lastrić

Špansko D.Cesarići 35 Zagreb tel/fax: 385 (1) 37 91 595

Client:
Poliklinika Lastric
Nature of Business:
Abdominal surgery clinic
Design Firm:
Cavar & Sefic
Art Director:
Lana Cavar
Designers:
Lana Cavar, Damir Sefic

Client:
Furniture Options
Nature of Business:
Rental furnishings
Design Firm:
Greteman Group
Art Directors:
Sonia Greteman, James Strange

Client:
Koch Crime Commission
Nature of Business:
Public safety
Design Firm:
Greteman Group
Art Directors:
Sonia Greteman, James Strange

Client:
Shorts International Film Festival
Design Firm:
Viva Dolan Communications +
Design
Art Director:
Frank Viva
Designer:
Sara Purves
Illustrator:
Sara Purves

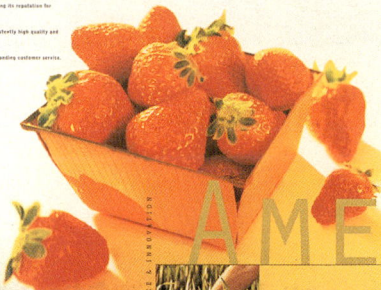

Client:
Services Group of America
Design Firm:
Hornall Anderson Design Works, Inc
Art Director:
Jack Anderson
Designers:
Jack Anderson, Julie Lock,
Heidi Favour

Client:
Towers Perrin
Nature of Business:
Human resources consulting
Design Firm:
Toni Schowalter Design
Art Director:
Toni Schowalter
Illustrator:
Toni Schowalter

Client:
Four Seeds Corporation, Japan
Nature of Business:
Corporate sports club
Design Firm:
Tom Fowler, Inc.
Art Directors:
Elizabeth P. Ball, Thomas G. Fowler
Designer:
Thomas G. Fowler
Illustrator:
Thomas G. Fowler

PIZZA-LA

OCEAN SPORTS CLUB

Client:
Crown Printing
Design Firm:
Nice Ltd.
Art Director:
Davide Nicosia

Client:
Iowa State Fair
Design Firm:
Sayles Graphic Design
Art Director:
John Sayles
Illustrator:
John Sayles

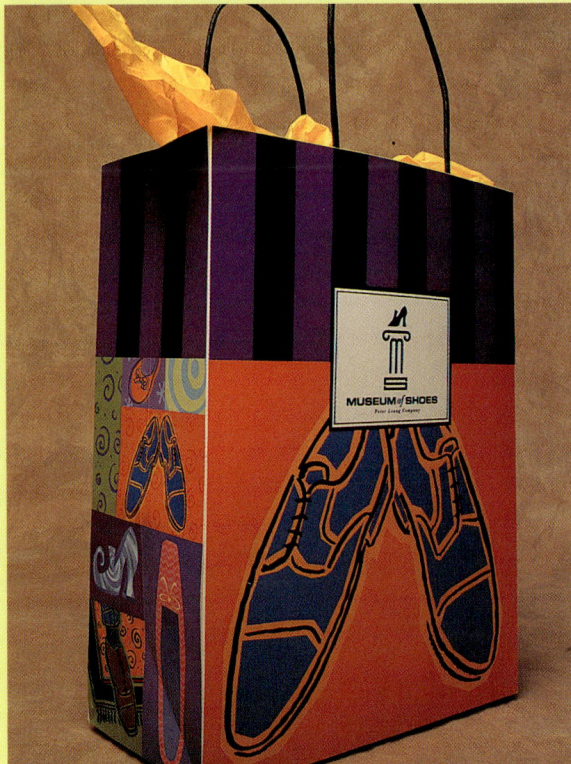

Client:
Peter Leung Company
Nature of Business:
Department Store
Design Firm:
Supon Design Group
Art Directors:
Supon Phornirunlit, Maria Sese-Paul
Designers:
Sharisse Steber, Maria Sese-Paul,
Jeanette J. Nelson

Client:
Newer Technology, Inc.
Nature of Business:
Computer
Design Firm:
Insight Design Communications
Art Directors:
Sherrie and Tracy Holdeman
Designers:
Chris Parks, Sherrie and Tracy
Holdeman
Illustrators:
Chris Parks, Sherrie and Tracy
Holdeman

Client:
Sagacho Exhibit Space
Nature of Business:
Music concert
Design Firm:
Design Club Inc.
Art Director:
Katsuhiro Kinoshita

Client:
Public Art
Nature of Business:
City advisory board
Design Firm:
Greteman Group
Art Directors:
Sonia Greteman, James Strange

Client:
Kraft Foods Limited
Nature of Business:
Food manufacture
Design Firm:
Asprey Di Donato Design P/L
Art Director:
Asprey Di Donato Design
Illustrator:
Mark Sofilas

Client:
Taylor Guitars
Nature of Business:
Acoustic guitar manufacture
Design Firm:
Mires Design, Inc.
Art Director:
Scott Mires
Designers:
Scott Mires, Miguel Perez

Client:
Croatian Government
Nature of Business:
International promotion
Design Firm:
Studio International
Art Director:
Boris Ljubicic
Illustrator:
Oleg Ivanisevic
Photographer
Boris Ljubicic

Client:
Virtual Celebrity Productions
Nature of Business:
Celebrity computer generation
Design Firm:
Insight Design Communications
Art Directors:
Sherrie and Tracy Holdeman
Illustrators:
Sherrie and Tracy Holdeman

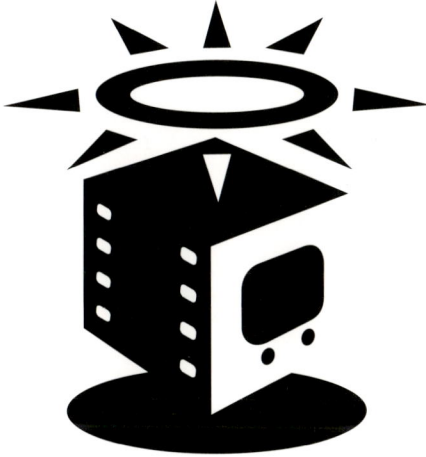

Client:
Perfectly Round Productions
Nature of Business:
Film/video production
Design Firm:
Greteman Group
Art Director:
Sonia Greteman

Client:
Clothes The Deal
Nature of Business:
Clothing
Design Firm:
Shimokochi/Reeves
Art Directors:
Mamoru Shimokochi, Anne Reeves
Designer:
Mamoru Shimokochi

Client:
Corundum International
Nature of Business:
Gem dealership
Design Firm:
Eclipse
Art Director:
Byron Jacobs

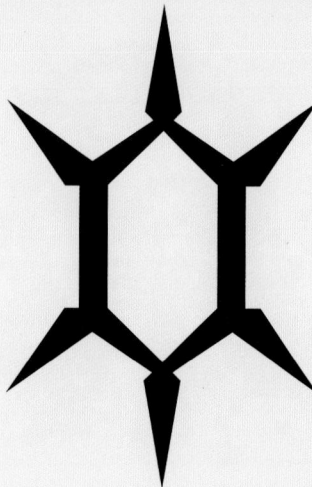

Client:
Island Dental Professionals
Nature of Business:
Dentistry
Design Firm:
VOICE Design
Art Director:
Clifford Cheng
Illustrator:
Clifford Cheng

Client:
Scottsdale Memorial Health System
Nature of Business:
Health care
Design Firm:
SHR Perceptual Management
Designer:
Nathan Joseph

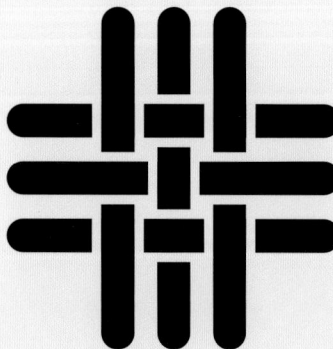

Client:
Ricochet Creative Thinking
Nature of Business:
Design and advertising
Design Firm:
Ricochet Creative Thinking
Art Director:
Steve Zelle

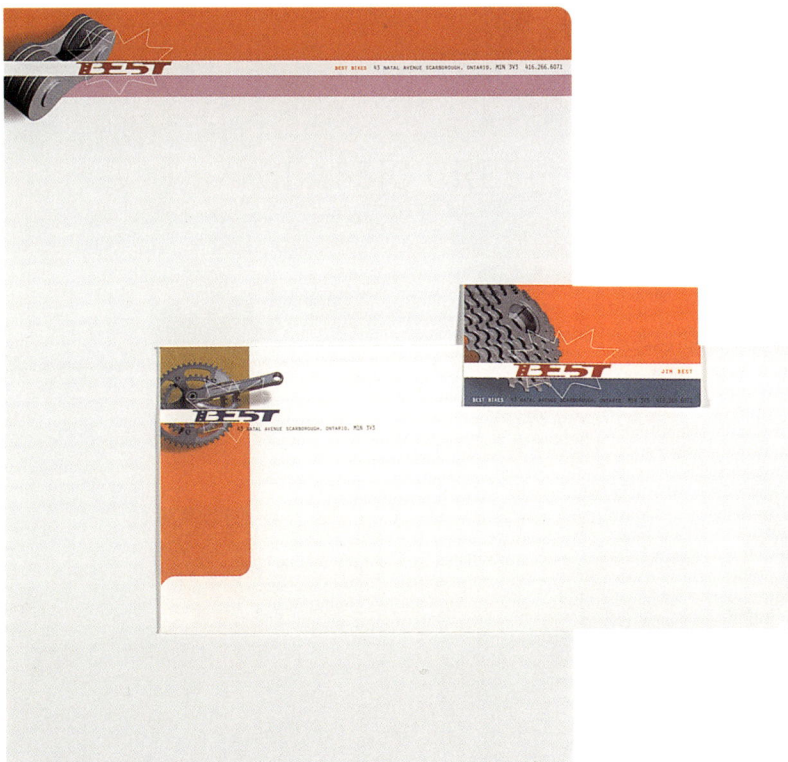

Client:
Best Bikes
Nature of Business:
Custom bike manufacture
Design Firm:
Overdrive Design
Art Directors:
James Wilson, Jay Wilson
Designers:
James Wilson, Jay Wilson, Terry Lau
Illustrator:
Dan Rempel

Client:
Protection Mutual
Nature of Business:
Property insurance
Design Firm:
Michael Stanard, Inc.
Art Directors:
Michael Stanard, Marc Fuhrman
Designer:
Kristy Vandekerckhove

ANNUAL REPORT 1996

PROTECTION.
IT'S OUR
WORD.

PROTECTION MUTUAL INSURANCE COMPANY

A WISE MAN WILL MAKE
MORE OPPORTUNITIES
THAN HE FINDS.

— FRANCIS BACON

INTERNATIONAL

Client:
China Int'l Travel Service HK Ltd
Design Firm:
Ken & Lau Design Consultants
Art Directors:
Kan Tai-keung, Freeman Lau, Eddy Yu
Designer:
Veronica Chung

Client:
Hill Ave. Drugs
Nature of Business:
Pharmacy
Design Firm:
Bradbury Design Inc.
Art Director:
Catharine Bradbury

Client:
Four-1-1 Corporation
Nature of Business:
Free e-mail for the world
Design Firm:
Stowe Design
Art Director:
Jodie Stowe

Client:
Compass Licensing
Nature of Business:
Licensing
Design Firm:
Visual Marketing Associates
Art Director:
Tracy Meiners

DAVID GOUBEAUX
President

Client:
Acumen Group
Nature of Business:
Marketing consulting
Design Firm:
Sayles Graphic Design
Art Director:
John Sayles
Illustrator:
John Sayles

725 Cowper Street, Suite 45 • Palo Alto, California 94301 • (415) 326-8117 Fax (415) 321-8111 • Internet bwqc20a@prodigy.com

ACUMEN
GROUP

725 Cowper Street, Suite 45 • Palo Alto, California 94301

ACUMEN
GROUP

London • Portland •   "MARKETING YOUR PRODUCTS TO THE WORLD"   • San Francisco • Santiago

Client:
Big Brothers & Sisters
Nature of Business:
Annual bowling event
Design Firm:
Greteman Group
Art Directors:
Sonia Greteman, James Strange

Client:
Fusion Media
Nature of Business:
Multimedia development
Design Firm:
Mires Design, Inc.
Art Director:
John Ball
Designers:
John Ball, Deborah Hom

Client:
Association for Information and
Image Management International
Nature of Business:
Document management
Design Firm:
Dever Designs, Inc.
Art Director:
Jeffrey L. Dever

Client:
Vision Center
Nature of Business:
Eye bank and research
Design Firm:
Zamboo
Designer:
Becca Bootes

Client:
Dogloo
Nature of Business:
International pet product
manufacture
Design Firm:
Zamboo
Designers:
Dave Zambotti, Becca Bootes

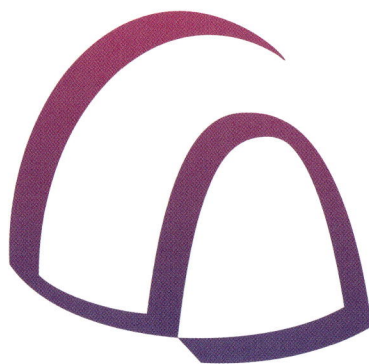

Client:
National Cancer Institute/Matthews
Media Group, Inc.
Nature of Business:
Cancer research
Design Firm:
Alphawave Designs
Art Director:
Douglas Dunbebin
Illustrator:
Douglas Dunbebin

Client:
Performance Graphique
Nature of Business:
Printing
Design Firm:
Studio Première Impression
Designer:
Mance Raby

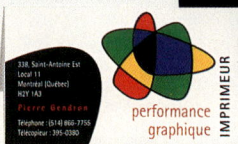

performance
graphique IMPRIMEUR

338, Saint-Antoine Est
Local 11
Montréal (Québec)
H2Y 1A3

Pierre Gendron

Téléphone : (514) 860-7755
Télécopieur : 395-0380

performance
graphique IMPRIMEUR

performance
graphique IMPRIMEUR

338, Saint-Antoine Est
Local 11
Montréal (Québec)
H2Y 1A3

Téléphone : (514) 860-7755
Télécopieur : 395-0380

Client:
The Gene Machine
Nature of Business:
Recruitment
Design Firm:
Hugonnet Design Associates
Art Director:
Rebecca Hugonnet
Illustrator:
David Welch

The **Gene** Machine™

The **Gene** Machine™

GABRIELLE CURTIN
Business Principal

The Gene Machine (Aust) Pty Limited
Level 3, 3 Wellington Street
Windsor Victoria 3181
Telephone (03) 9521 4422
Facsimile (03) 9521 4049

The Gene Machine (Vic) Pty Ltd
Level 3, 3 Wellington Street
Windsor Victoria 3181
Telephone (03) 9521 4422
Facsimile (03) 9521 4049
ACN 075 138 195

Client:
Envelope Manager Software
Nature of Business:
Mail automation
Design Firm:
Stowe Design
Art Director:
Jodie Stowe

ENVELOPE
MANAGER
S O F T W A R E

Client:
The Floating Gallery
Nature of Business:
Art photography exhibition
Design Firm:
Brown Communications Group
Art Director:
Morris Antosh
Designer:
Tom Chaput
Illustrator:
Tom Chaput

Client:
Charles Schwab/Marjorie Gross and
Company, Inc.
Nature of Business:
Financial consulting
Design Firm:
Tom Dolle Design
Art Director:
Tom Dolle

ON THE
JOB
@
SCHWAB

Client:
Fernando & Partners
Nature of Business:
Advertising planning
Design Firm:
Hoyne Design
Art Director:
Andrew Hoyne

Client:
Futures For Children
Nature of Business:
Film festival
Design Firm:
Kilmer & Kilmer
Art Director:
Richard Kilmer
Designer:
Randall Marshall

Client:
Raytheon
Design firm:
Insight Design
Art Directors:
Emily A. Gallardo,
Tracy and Sherrie Holdeman

Infrastructure

Metals and Mining

Government

Transportation

Power

Fabrication

Environmental Services

Nuclear

people's bank

http://www.peoples.com

1996 Annual Report

Client:
People's Bank
Design Firm:
Ted Bertz Graphic Design, Inc
Art Director:
Ted Bertz
Designers:
Ted Bertz, Mark Terranova
Photographer:
Ted Kawalerski

Hard Hats

In 1996 People's

ENTERPRISE

■ Was the Connecticut Development Authority's most active lender

■ Continued our commitment to community-based economic projects, including the $61 million Bank on Bridgeport revitalization plan

■ Increased average commercial checking deposits by 14%

■ Increased the commercial loan portfolio 11%

■ Grew commercial-related fee-based revenues 16%

Longshoremen from left to right: William J. O'Neill III, William Miller, David Shula, Joe Russo, Thomas Estabrook.

Client:
The Roasterie, Inc.
Nature of Business:
Coffee sales and roasting
Design Firm:
McMillian Design
Art Director:
William McMillian
Illustrator:
William McMillian

Client:
The Food Boys Restaurant
Design Firm:
George Peters Design & Illustration
Art Director:
George Peters
Illustrator:
George Peters

Client:
Just Joe Coffee Carts
Design Firm:
Fine Design Group
Art Director:
Kenn Fine
Illustrator:
Kenn Fine

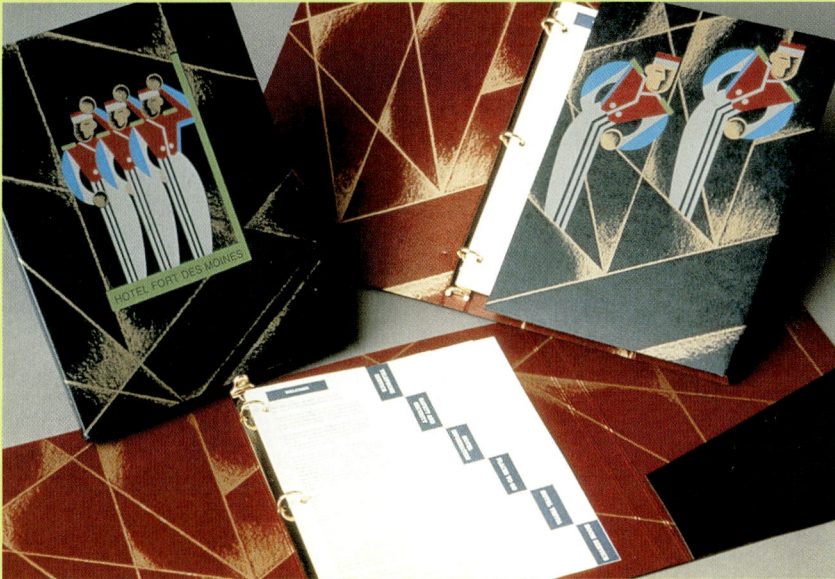

Client:
Hotel Fort Des Moines
Design Firm:
Sayles Graphic Design
Art Director:
John Sayles
Illustrator:
John Sayles

Client:
Prairie Print
Nature of Business:
Screen printing
Design Firm:
Insight Design Communications
Art Directors:
Sherrie and Tracy Holdeman
Illustrators:
Sherrie and Tracy Holdeman

Client:
Ken Coit Video
Nature of Business:
Video design and production
Design Firm:
McMillian Design
Art Director:
William McMillian
Illustrator:
William McMillian

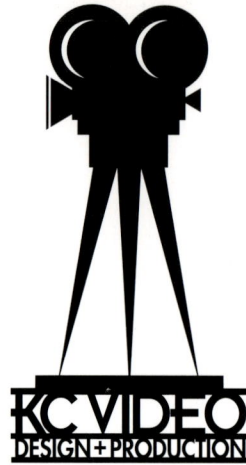

Client:
Potomac Polymer Clay Guild
Nature of Business:
Polymer clay art
Design Firm:
Dever Designs, Inc.
Art Director:
Jeffrey L. Dever

Client:
Pomurski sejem
Nature of Business:
Fruit fair
Design Firm:
KROG
Art Director:
Edi Berk

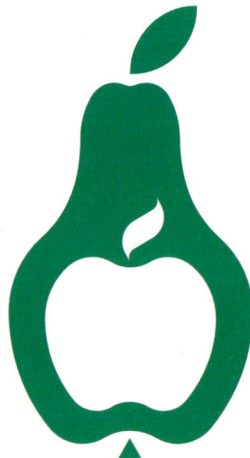

Client:
Overdrive Design
Nature of Business:
Graphic design and multimedia
Design Firm:
Overdrive Design
Art Director:
James Wilson
Illustrator:
James Wilson

Client:
Portfolio Center
Nature of Business:
Design school
Design Firm:
Oxygen, Inc.
Designer:
Penina A. Goodman
Photographer:
Horace J. Hicks

Client:
Orduña Design
Nature of Business:
Jewelry design
Design Firm:
BRD Design
Art Director:
Peter King Robbins

Client:
Nikki Goldstein
Nature of Business:
Beauty writing
Design Firm:
Hoyne Design
Art Director:
Andrew Hoyne
Designers:
Andrew Hoyne,
Amanda McPherson
Photographer:
Rob Blackburn

Client:
Moisturelock
Design Firm:
Greteman Group
Art Director:
Sonia Greteman

Client:
Creative Nail Design
Nature of Business:
Cosmetic botanical oil
Design Firm:
Kahn Design
Art Director:
Jeff Kahn

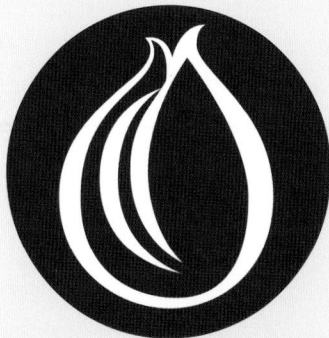

ORDUÑA

DESIGN

Client:
Orduña Design
Nature of Business:
Jewelry Design
Design Firm:
BRD Design
Art Director:
Peter King Robbins

Client:
Trail Head
Nature of Business:
Outwear clothing
Design Firm:
Swieter Design U.S.
Art Director:
John Swieter
Designer:
Mark Ford

Client:
Cohabaco Cigar Company
Design Firm:
Sayles Graphic Design
Art Director:
John Sayles
Illustrator:
John Sayles

Client:
CareScape
Nature of Business:
Landscape maintenance and
contracting
Design Firm:
Richardson or Richardson
Art Director:
Forrest Richardson
Designer:
Nathan Taylor
Illustrator:
Nathan Taylor

CareScape

Client:
Redo House and Garden
Nature of Business:
Home and garden retail
Design Firm:
Overdrive Design
Art Directors:
James Wilson, Jay Wilson
Designer:
Jay Wilson
Illustrator:
Jay Wilson

Client:
Indigo at Great Falls
Nature of Business:
Restaurant
Design Firm:
Supon Design Group
Art Director:
Khoi Vinh
Designer:
Soung Wiser

Client:
Bio 90 Manufacturing Inc.
Nature of Business:
Biodegradable cleaning products
Design Firm:
The Riordan Design Group Inc.
Art Director:
Ric Riordan
Designer:
Sharon Pece

Client:
American Institute of Wine & Food
Nature of Business:
Trade organization
Design Firm:
Toni Schowalter Design
Art Director:
Toni Schowalter
Illustrator:
Toni Schowalter

Client:
Seton Hall University
College of Arts and Sciences
Design Firm:
Seton Hall University
Publications Office
Art Director:
Jean Smith
Designer:
Umberto Fusco
Illustrator:
Umberto Fusco

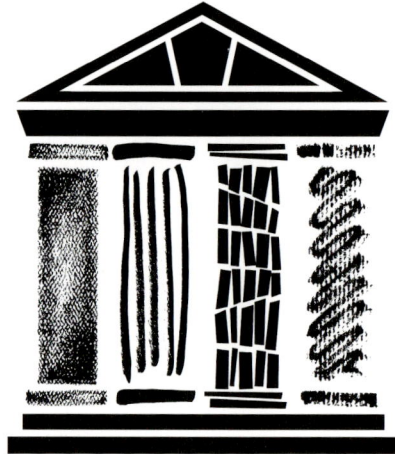

Client:
Calvary Chapel
Nature of Business:
Church Café
Design Firm:
Kilmer & Kilmer
Art Director:
Richard Kilmer
Designer:
Randall Marshall

Client:
Dubrulle
Nature of Business:
French Culinary School
Design Firm:
Fleming Design Group
Art Director:
Blair Pocock
Designer:
Darren Bristol
Illustrator:
Michael Knox

Client:
Cook in the Closet
Nature of Business:
Catering
Design Firm:
Cozzolino Ellett Design D'Vision
Art Director:
Darren Ledwich

Client:
Viacom
Nature of Business:
Entertainment retail
Design Firm:
Tom Dolle Design
Art Directors:
Tom Dolle, Linda Espinosa
Designer:
Chris Riely

Client:
Food Group/Boyds Coffee
Nature of Business:
Food and beverage
Design Firm:
Mires Design, Inc.
Art Directors:
Scott Mires, Mike Brower
Designers:
Mike Brower, Scott Mires
Illustrator:
Tracy Sabin

Client:
Viacom
Nature of Business:
Entertainment retail
Design Firm:
Tom Dolle Design
Art Directors:
Tom Dolle, Linda Espinosa
Designer:
Jana Paterson

Client:
Jamba Juice
Nature of Business:
Fresh juice sales
Design Firm:
Hornall Anderson Design Works, Inc.
Art Director:
Jack Anderson
Designers:
Jack Anderson, Lisa Cerveny,
Suzanne Haddon
Illustrator:
Mits Katayama

Client:
Street 20
Nature of Business:
Street kids welfare
Design Firm:
Cozzolino Ellett Design D'Vision
Art Director:
Darren Ledwich
Illustrators:
Darren Ledwich, Mike McHugh

Client:
Wordsworth, Inc.
Nature of Business:
Copywriting
Design Firm:
Fuszion Art + Design
Art Director:
Tony Fletcher

Client:
Cherry Print
Nature of Business:
Offset printing
Design Firm:
Marcus Lee Design Pty Ltd
Art Director:
Marcus Lee
Designer:
George Margaritis

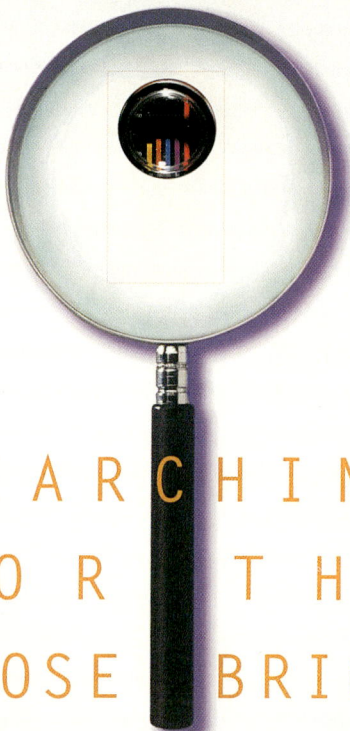

EXECUTIVE RISK

1995 ANNUAL REPORT

SEARCHING FOR THE LOOSE BRICK

Client:
Executive Risk, Inc.
Nature of Business:
Reinsurance
Design Firm:
Ted Bertz Graphic Design
Art Director:
Ted Bertz
Designers:
Ted Bertz, Mimi LaPoint,
Scott Kuykendall
Photographer:
Paul Horton
Imager:
Jim Coon Studio

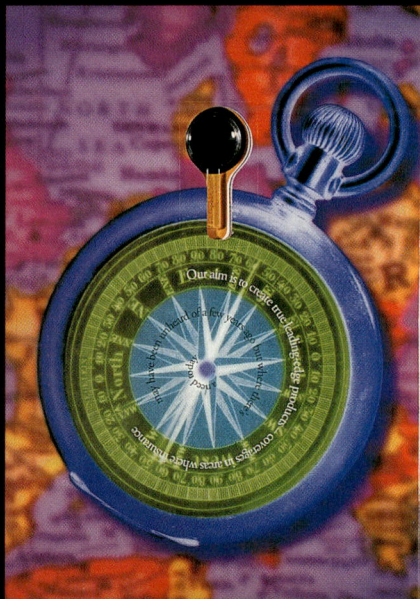

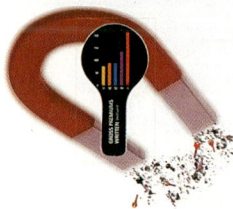

Creating Value

The 1990s have been a period characterized by dramatic change within the insurance industry, a time when many insurers have been understandably reticent to make predictions or promises about anything. Yet, in last year's loose bricks Annual Report, Executive Risk's management did make a promise. After describing an absolutely kinetic 1994, which had been dominated by a series of significant corporate developments (acquiring full control of our underwriting company, Executive Risk Management Associates, and the initial public offering of our common stock), we declared: "Executive Risk's people [are] poised to move beyond transitional issues and into a full four quarters of concentrating on our strengths — searching out and seizing the opportunities that the executive and professional liability markets present and profiting in the process." There, in one sentence, the 1994 Annual Report capsulated the two real benchmarks that investors can use to evaluate the success of our Company's loose bricks underwriting philosophy: entrepreneurial vigilance and underwriting for profit.

So, how did we do? As you've already read in Roy Vander Putten's and Bob Kullas' letter to shareholders, the Company's 1995 fiscal year was an excellent financial success. Net operating earnings were up significantly during the year, and that benefited the Company's stock price, which more than doubled between January 1 and December 31. The Company finished the year with a 95.5% GAAP combined ratio, a key measure of operating efficiency. As we've explained in the past, a combined ratio under 100% is a positive result, indicating the achievement of an underwriting profit. Our 1995 combined ratio proves that, once again, Executive Risk

Client:
Burke Corp.
Nature of Business:
Various food products
Design Firm:
Gardner Design
Art Director:
Bill Gardner
Illustrator:
Dave LaFleur

PREMORO ®

TEZZATA ®

MAGNIFOODS ®

Client:
S'Apori D'Italia UK Ltd.
Nature of Business:
Italian delicacies
Design Firm:
The Ian Logan Design Company
Art Director:
Alan Colville
Designer:
Rita Palmieri
Illustrator:
Roy Knipe

Client:
The Sisyphus Enterprise
Nature of Business:
Gift products
Design Firm:
Michael Stanard, Inc.
Art Director:
Michael Stanard
Designers:
Kristy Vandekerckhove,
Michael Stanard

Client:
Phil Rudy Photography
Nature of Business:
Photography
Design Firm:
Shields Design
Art Director:
Charles Shields
Photographer:
Phil Rudy

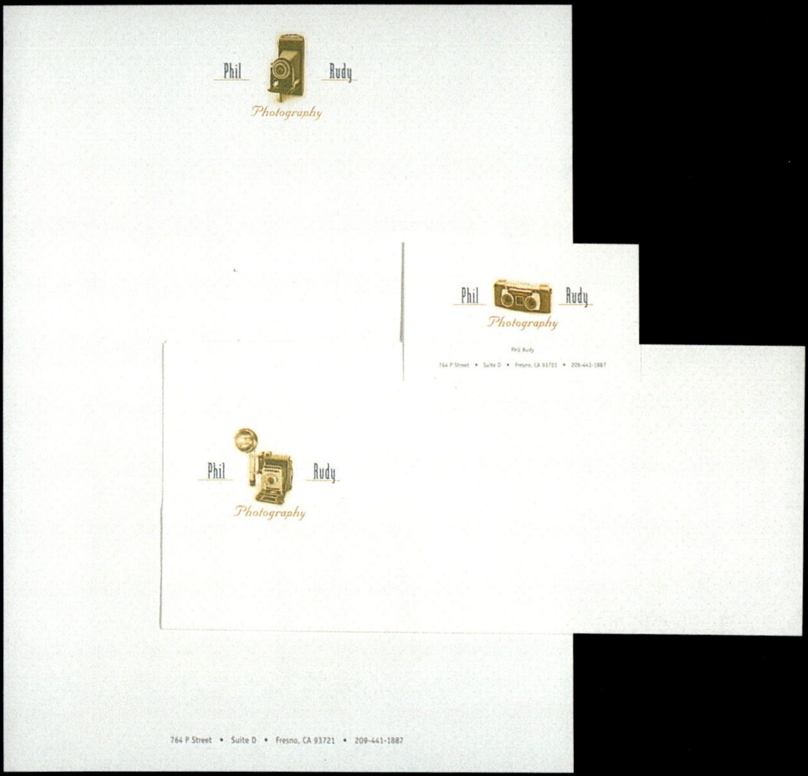

Client:
Patrick Harbron
Nature of Business:
Photography
Design Firm:
Viva Dolan Communications +
Design
Art Director:
Frank Viva
Designer:
James Ryce

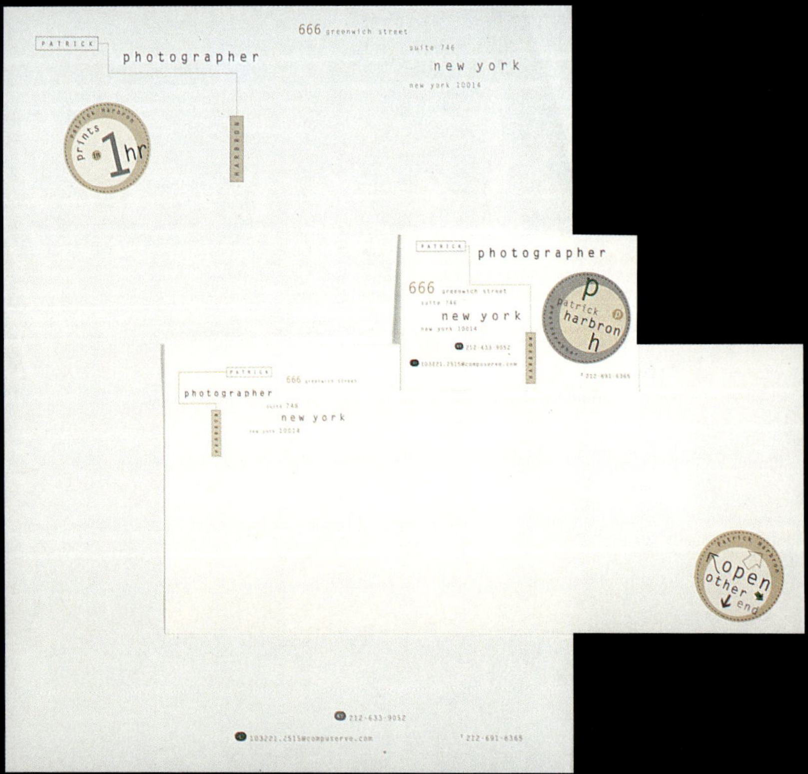

Le Desktop®

Client:
Le Desktop
Nature of Business:
Catalog desktop accessories
Design Firm:
Richardson or Richardson
Art Director:
Forrest Richardson
Illustrator:
Kee Rash

MINIMAX

Client:
Minimax
Nature of Business:
Homeware retail
Design Firm:
Cozzolino Ellett Design D'Vision
Art Director:
Phil Ellett
Illustrator:
Mike McHugh

COZY COUNTRYSIDE
COUNSELING

Client:
Debbie Krause
Nature of Business:
Individual and family counseling
Design Firm:
Simantel Group
Art Director:
Wendy Behrens
Illustrator:
Lisa Lucas

Client:
AIGA - New York
Nature of Business:
Design
Design Firm:
J. Graham Hanson Design
Art Director:
J. Graham Hanson
Designers:
J. Graham Hanson, Iris Teo

A Night at the Movies

Client:
Crews Protective Eyewear
Nature of Business:
Eyewear/safety glasses
Design Firm:
Perdue Creative
Art Director:
Jay Perdue
Designer:
Lisa Jo Perdue

FROSTBITE

Client:
The California Endowment
Nature of Business:
Grant foundation
Design Firm:
Casper Design Group
Art Director:
Bill Ribar
Designer:
Daniel McClain
Illustrator:
Daniel McClain

THE CALIFORNIA ENDOWMENT

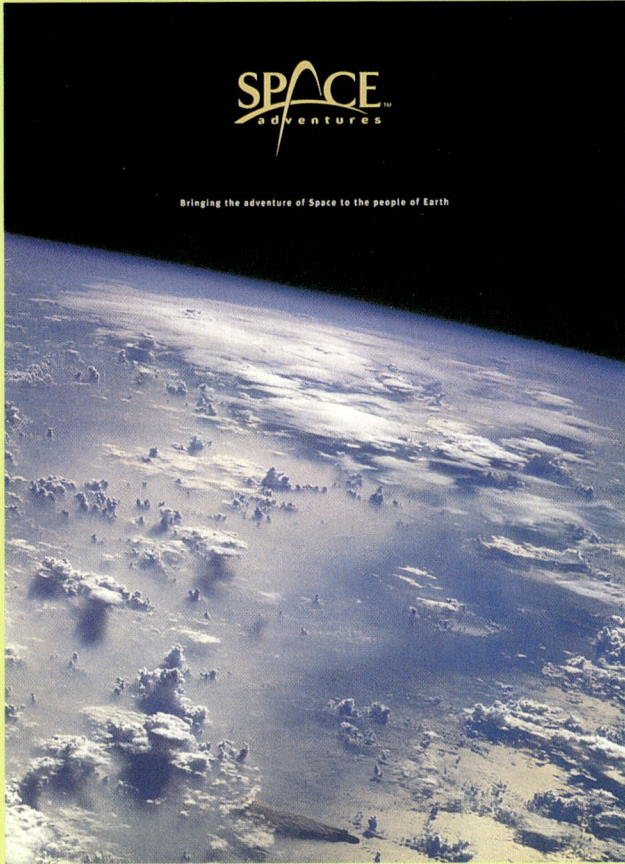

Bringing the adventure of Space to the people of Earth

Client:
Space Adventures
Nature of Business:
Travel
Design Firm:
Supon Design Group
Art Directors:
Supon Phornirunlit,
Jacques Coughlin
Designer:
Saundrea Cika

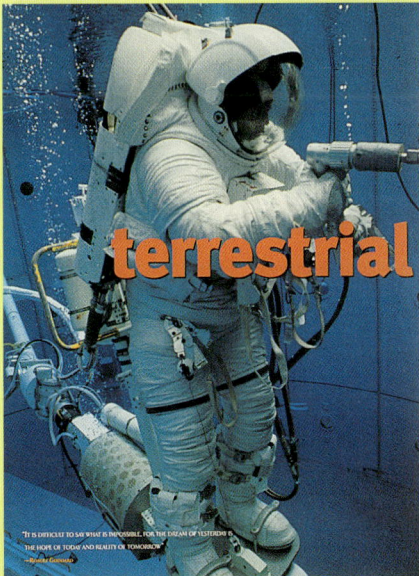

Client:
Agassi Enterprises
Nature of Business:
Sports gripping powder retail
Design Firm:
Mires Design, Inc.
Art Director:
Jose A. Serrano
Photographer:
Carl Vanderschuit

Client:
Nell Baking Company
Nature of Business:
Gourmet cookies
Design Firm:
Lambert Design
Art Director:
Christie Lambert
Photographer:
James Elliott

Starbucks Corporation

1995 Annual Report

Client:
Starbucks Coffee Company
Nature of Business:
Coffee and specialty product retail
Design Firm:
Hornall Anderson Design Works, Inc.
Art Director:
Jack Anderson
Designers:
Jack Anderson, Julie Lock,
Heidi Favour
Photographer:
Alan Abramowitz, stock photos

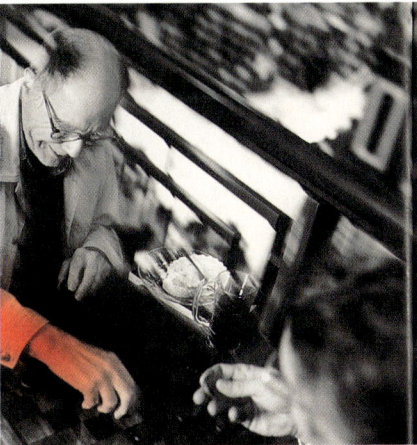

[Accessible / Irrepressible]

It's incredible when you think of the many different ways we reach people every day. Look, up in the air! You'll find Starbucks at 22,000 feet on Horizon Airlines, and soon, on United worldwide. (And in 49 airport kiosks via Host Marriott nationwide.) We're here, in your mailbox and at home thanks to our Mail Order division. And here, when you shop at Nordstrom or Barnes & Noble, or check into one of 46 ITT Sheraton hotels. Even here, at sea, wherever the ships of Holland America Line sail, Starbucks is along. Familiar... comforting... readily accessible. To keep up with this astonishing growth, and indeed, open up even greater possibilities, we kicked off operations at our first East Coast distribution and roasting facility in York, Pennsylvania this September. So stay tuned. Enjoying Starbucks is getting easier all the time. If you're looking for a great cup of coffee, we might just find you.

Client:
Grant Telegraph
Nature of Business:
Historic condominiums
Design Firm:
Greteman Group
Art Directors:
Sonia Greteman, James Strange

Client:
Geo Furniture
Design Firm:
Hoyne Design
Art Director:
Andrew Hoyne
Designers:
Angela Ho, Andrew Hoyne
Illustrator:
Angela Ho

Client:
House Communications
Nature of Business:
Public relations
Design Firm:
Swieter Design U.S.
Art Director:
John Swieter
Designer:
Julie Poth

Client:
Grant Telegraph Centre
Nature of Business:
Historic condominiums
Design Firm:
Greteman Group
Art Directors:
Sonia Greteman, James Strange

Client:
Lighthouse Communications
Nature of Business:
Market support/public relations
Design Firm:
Meta 4
Art Director:
Meta 4

Client:
Roaring Tiger Films
Nature of Business:
Film production
Design Firm:
DogStar
Art Director:
Jennifer Martin
Illustrator:
Rodney Davidson

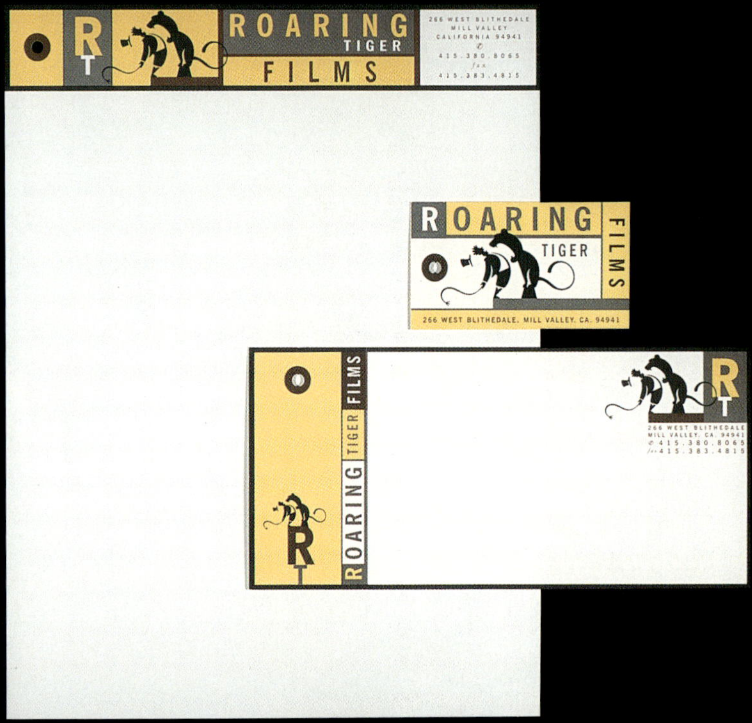

Client:
Sizuka
Nature of Business:
Japanese confectionery
Design Firm:
Design Club Inc.
Art Director:
Katsuhiro Kinoshita

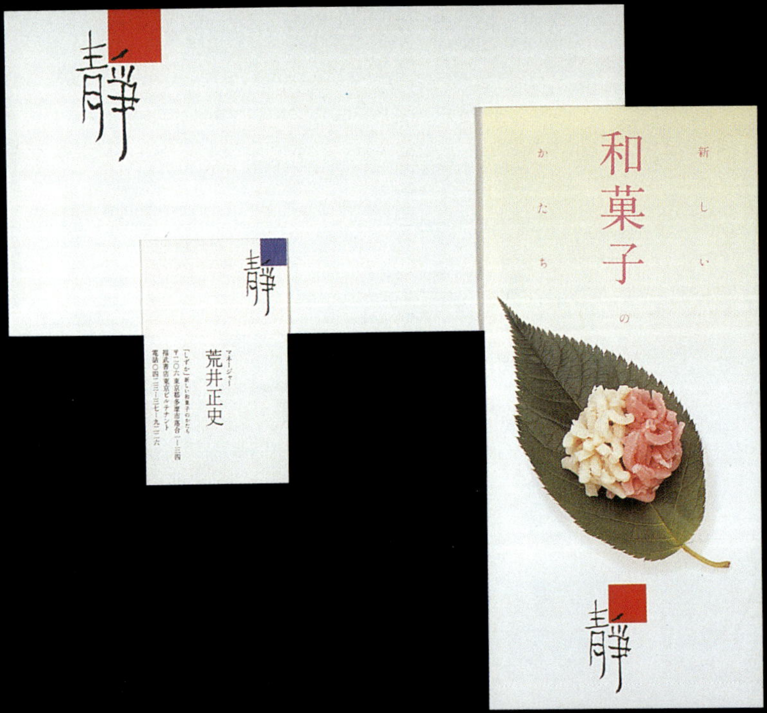

Client:
Regional Council, Hong Kong
Nature of Business:
Poster Exhibition
Design Firm:
Kan & Lau Design Consultants
Art Director:
Freeman Lau Siu Hong

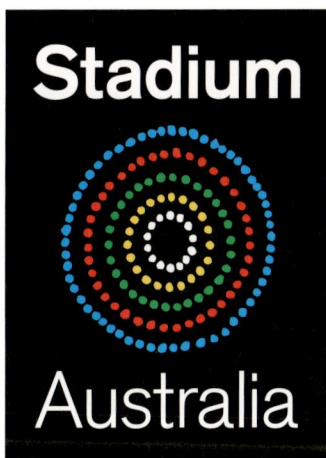

Client:
Stadium Australia
Nature of Business:
Construction and Management
of Olympic Stadium
Design Firm:
Horniak & Canny
Art Director:
Robyn Wakefield

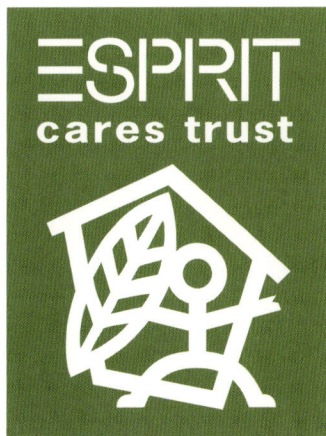

Client:
Esprit Cares Trust Fund
Nature of Business:
Fundraising project
Design Firm:
Hoyne Design
Art Director:
Andrew Hoyne
Illustrator:
Hoyne Design

Client:
Piping & Equipment Co., Inc.
Nature of Business:
Industrial piping contracting
Design Firm:
Greteman Group
Art Directors:
Sonia Greteman, James Strange

Client:
Cafe Barcelona
Nature of Business:
Spanish restaurant
Design Firm:
Hoyne Design
Art Director:
Andrew Hoyne
Illustrator:
Angela Ho

Client:
Jam Lady Jam
Nature of Business:
Jam Manufacture
Design Firm:
Hoyne Design
Art Director:
Andrew Hoyne
Illustrator:
Angela Ho

Client:
Pia Corporation
Nature of Business:
Cartoon character applications
Design Firm:
Kirima Design Office
Art Director:
Harumi Kirima
Designers:
Harumi Kirima, Fumitaka Yukawa

Client:
Old Town Association of Wichita
Nature of Business:
Annual event
Design Firm:
Insight Design Communications
Art Directors:
Sherrie and Tracy Holdeman
Illustrators:
Sherrie and Tracy Holdeman

Client:
US West Communications
Nature of Business:
Telecommunications
Design Firm:
Vaughn/Wedeen Creative

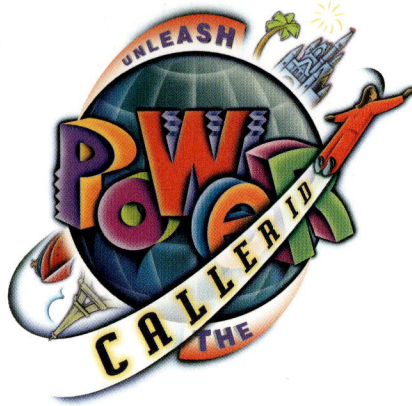

Client:
Willy Hair Wizzard
Nature of Business:
Hair stylist
Design Firm:
Fine Design Group
Art Director:
Kenn Fine
Designer:
Jake Barlow
Illustrator:
Jake Barlow

Client:
Michael Bone Photography
Nature of Business:
Photography
Design Firm:
Marcus Lee Design Pty Ltd
Art Director:
Marcus Lee
Designer:
George Margaritis

Client:
Gary Pember
Nature of Business:
Strategic marketing
Design Firm:
Insight Design Communications
Art Directors:
Sherrie and Tracy Holdeman
Illustrators:
Sherrie and Tracy Holdeman

Client:
Kansas State University
Nature of Business:
Department of Entomology
Design Firm:
Gardner Design
Art Director:
Brian Miller
Illustrator:
Brian Miller

Client:
Micky Wilson
Nature of Business:
CD ROM software
Design Firm:
Franklin Templeton, Inc.
Art Director:
Micky Wilson
Designer:
Linda Kahn
Illustrator:
Linda Kahn

Client:
Vesta Dipping Grill
Nature of Business:
Restaurant
Design Firm:
Korn Design
Art Director:
Denise Korn
Designer:
Jenny Pelzek
Illustrator:
Jenny Pelzek

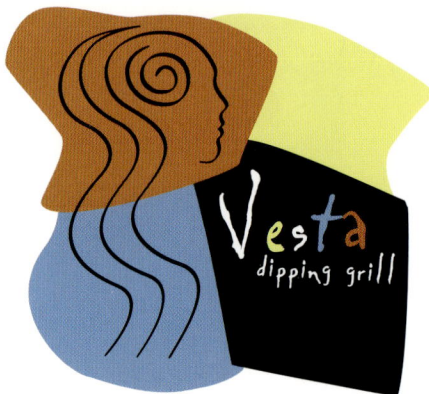

Client:
Southcorp Whitegoods
Nature of Business:
Whitegoods wholesale
Design Firm:
Marcus Lee Design Pty Ltd
Art Director:
Marcus Lee
Designer:
George Margaritis

Client:
RC Schmidt
Nature of Business:
Restaurant
Design Firm:
McDill Design
Designer:
Joel Harmeling
Illustrator:
Joel Harmeling

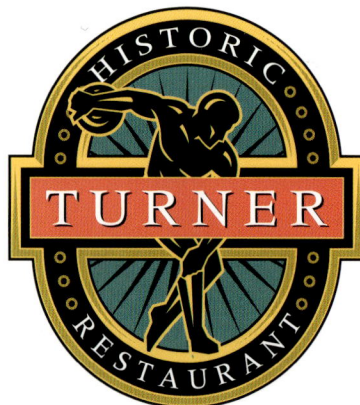

Client:
Perfectly Round Productions
Nature of Business:
TV show
Design Firm:
Insight Design Communications
Art Directors:
Sherrie and Tracy Holdeman
Illustrators:
Sherrie and Tracy Holdeman

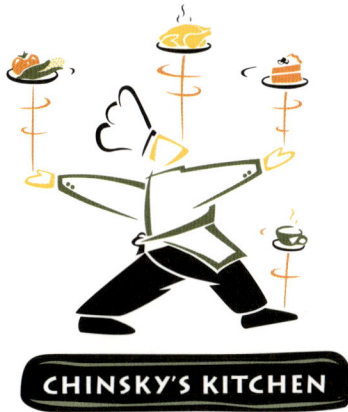

Client:
Chinsky's Kitchen
Nature of Business:
Restaurant
Design Firm:
Kiku Obata & Company
Art Director:
Joe Floresca
Illustrator:
Joe Floresca

Client:
D & B's Four Seasons Golf
Nature of Business:
Indoor golf range
Design Firm:
McDill Design
Art Director:
Joel Harmeling
Illustrator:
Joel Harmeling

Client:
VH1
Nature of Business:
Entertainment
Design Firm:
Parham Santana, Inc.
Art Directors:
Rick Tesoro, John Parham, Dean
Lubensky (VH1)
Project Manager:
Mary Russell (VH1)
Director:
Wayne Wilkins (VH1)
Designer:
Paula Kelly
Photographer:
Peter Medilek
Writer:
Adam Dolgins (VH1)

Client:
Fresh Paint
Nature of Business:
Faux finishing
Design Firm:
Insight Design Communications
Art Directors:
Sherrie and Tracy Holdeman
Illustrators:
Sherrie and Tracy Holdeman

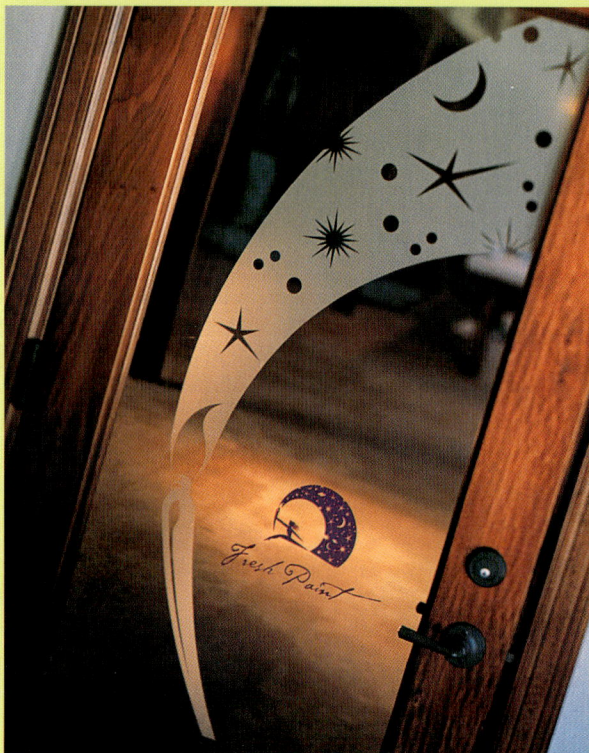

Client:
George Peters Design & Illustration
Nature of Business:
Humorous design
Design Firm:
George Peters Design & Illustration
Art Director:
George Peters
Illustrator:
George Peters

Client:
McDill Design
Nature of Business:
Design
Design Firm:
McDill Design
Art Director:
Michael Dillon
Designers:
Joel Harmeling, Michael Dillon
Illustrator:
Joel Harmeling

Client:
King of Noodles
Nature of Business:
Noodle cafe
Design Firm:
Hoyne Design
Art Director:
Andrew Hoyne
Designers:
Andrew Hoyne, Angela Ho
Illustrator:
Angela Ho

Client:
Gatehouse Montessori School
Design Firm:
Lindsay Simmonds Design
Art Director:
Matt Littledale
Designer:
Lindsay Simmonds
Illustrator:
Lindsay Simmonds

Client:
US Tennis Association
Nature of Business:
US Open Event
Design Firm:
Supon Design Group
Art Directors:
Supon Phornirunlit,
Brent Almond
Designer:
Jeanette Nelson

Client:
Department of Power
Nature of Business:
Power cycling spin studio
Design Firm:
Simple Green In-House Design
Art Director:
Mike Brower
Illustrator:
Mike Brower

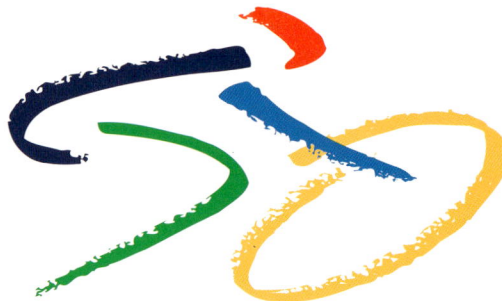

Client:
US West Communications
Nature of Business:
Telecommunications
Design Firm:
Vaughn/Wedeen Creative
Art Director:
Steve Wedeen

PUT THE PEDAL
TO THE METAL

W E
WINCAR ARE
DRIVEN
!
TURN ON THE POWER

We're telling you that this is the year to Turn On The Power! Well, we're turning it on, too! And we know of no more powerful way to encourage you to Put The Pedal To The Metal than by giving away a few new cars. Actually, more than a few. In 1997, we are power driven!

Client:
Pretty Good Privacy
Nature of Business:
Software encryption
Design Firm:
Hornall Anderson Design Works, Inc.
Art Director:
Jack Anderson
Designers:
Jack Anderson, Debra Hampton, Heidi
Favour, Jana Wilson

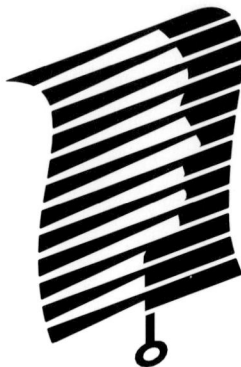

Client:
Face First
Nature of Business:
Facial salon
Design Firm:
Greteman Group
Art Director:
Sonia Greteman

Client:
Cigar Aficionado Magazine
Nature of Business:
Publishing
Design Firm:
DogStar
Art Director:
Martin Leeds
Designer:
Rodney Davidson
Illustrator:
Rodney Davidson

Client:
Levi Strauss & Co.
Nature of Business:
Fashion
Design Firm:
White Design, Inc.
Art Director:
Jamie Graupner

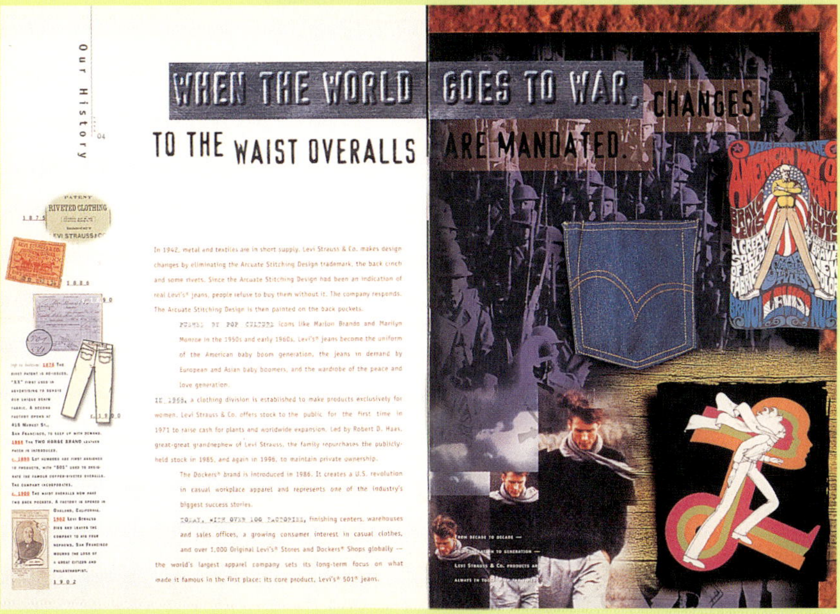

Client:
San Francisco Production Group
Nature of Business:
Video production
Design Firm:
Morla Design
Art Director:
Jennifer Morla
Designers:
Jennifer Morla, Craig Baily

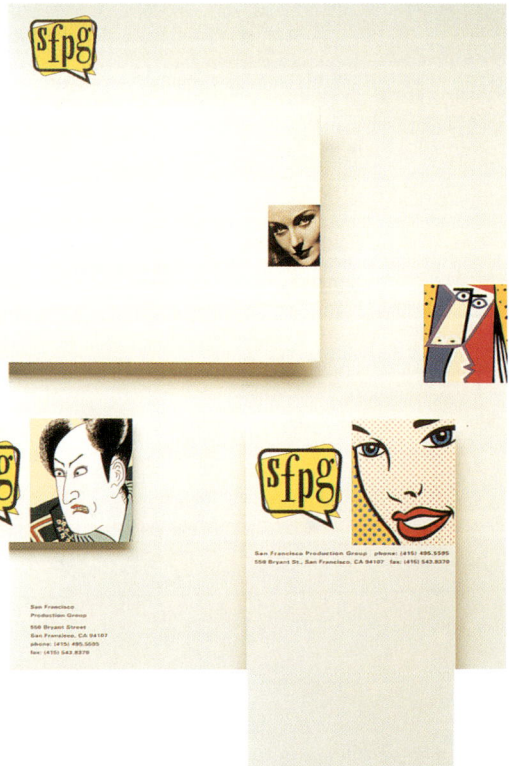

Brigitte no Rock

Client:
Brancaleone
Nature of Business:
Music festival
Design Firm:
Porto + Martinez Design Studio
Art Directors:
Bruno Porto, Marcelo Martinez
Designer:
Bruno Porto

Client:
Todd Adkins
Nature of Business:
Personal correspondence logos
Design Firm:
Born to Design
Art Director:
Todd Adkins
Illustrator:
Todd Adkins

Client:
Complete Post
Nature of Business:
Video post production
Design Firm:
Marcus Lee Pty Ltd
Art Director:
Marcus Lee
Designer:
Michelle Mackintosh

Client:
Herman Collins International
Nature of Business:
Executive recruitment
Design Firm:
Canary Studios
Designer:
Carrie English

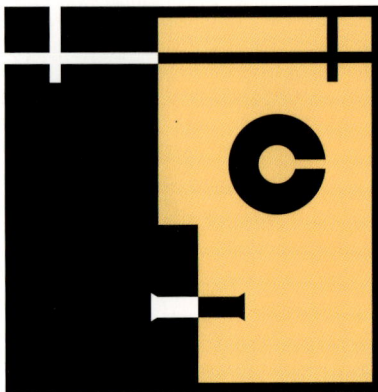

Client:
Obmocna obrtna zbornica Maribor
Nature of Business:
Craftsman association
Design Firm:
KROG
Art Director:
Edi Berk

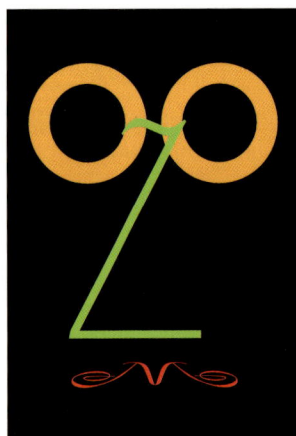

Client:
Futures for Children
Nature of Business:
Film festival
Design Firm:
Kilmer & Kilmer
Art Director:
Richard Kilmer
Designers:
Richard Kilmer, Randall Marshall

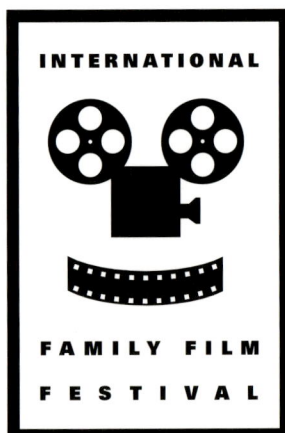

INTERNATIONAL

FAMILY FILM

FESTIVAL

Client:
Brite Voice Systems
Nature of Business:
Communications
Design Firm:
Greteman Group
Art Director:
Sonia Greteman

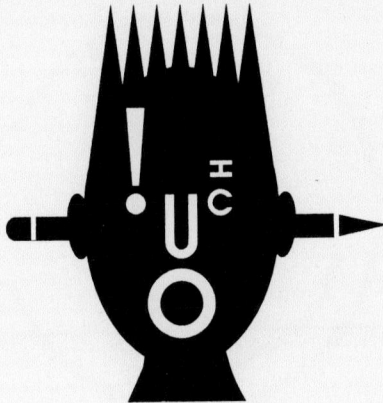

Client:
Ouch!
Nature of Business:
Design
Design Firm:
Greteman Group
Art Director:
James Strange

Client:
Rubo Records
Nature of Business:
Rap record company
Design Firm:
Insight Design Communications
Art Directors:
Sherrie and Tracy Holdeman
Illustrators:
Sherrie and Tracy Holdeman

Client:
City of Ballarat
Nature of Business:
Reunion event
Design Firm:
Peter Lambert Design
Art Director:
Peter Lambert
Designers:
Peter Lambert, Paul McKenna

Back to Ballarat 1998

Client:
James Elliott Photography
Nature of Business:
Photography
Design Firm:
Lambert Design
Art Director:
Christie Lambert
Designer:
Donna Smith

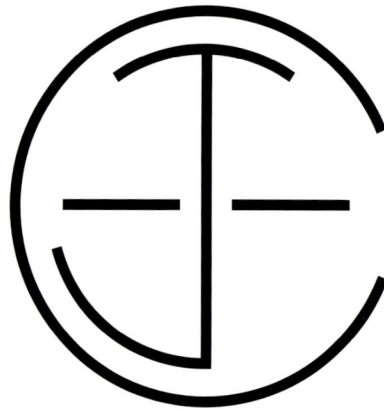

Client:
Satoshi Ifuji Supporters Association
Nature of Business:
Political advocacy
Design Firm:
Design Club Inc.
Art Director:
Katsuhiro Kinoshita

IFUJI SATOSHI

Client:
Manny's Heating, Cooling,
Air and Water
Nature of Business:
Environmental systems
Design Firm:
Greteman Group
Art Directors:
Sonia Greteman, James Strange

The Maritime **Aquarium**
AT NORWALK

Client:
The Maritime Aquarium of Norwalk
Nature of Business:
Public aquarium and museum
Design Firm:
Tom Fowler, Inc.
Art Director:
Thomas G. Fowler

Client:
Feat Australia
Nature of Business:
Student recruitment
Design Firm:
Marcus Lee Design Pty Ltd
Art Director:
Marcus Lee
Designer:
George Margaritis

Client:
Lance Endres
Nature of Business:
Design
Design Firm:
Endres Design
Art Director:
Lance Endres
Illustrator:
Lance Endres

Client:
Ocean World
Nature of Business:
Seafood and sushi bar
Design Firm:
Kojak Design
Designer:
Jack Harford
Illustrator:
Jack Harford

Client:
Alley Jams
Nature of Business:
Earth-friendly products
Design Firm:
Scorsone/Drueding
Art Directors:
Joe Scorsone, Alice Drueding
Illustrator:
Joe Scorsone

EARTH-FRIENDLY PRODUCTS

Client:
Sable Insurance Company
Nature of Business:
Property casualty insurance
Design Firm:
Driscoll Design
Art Director:
Terri Driscoll
Designers:
Terri Driscoll, Leslie Ruque

Client:
Gotcha
Nature of Business:
Clothing retail
Design Firm:
Mike Salisbury Communications
Art Director:
Mike Salisbury

Client:
Siskin Software
Nature of Business:
Software development
Design Firm:
Marlin Design
Art Director:
Declan Coughlan

Client:
Kristin and Tim Kelly
Nature of Business:
Wedding
Design Firm:
Jeff Fisher Logo Motives
Art Director:
Jeff Fisher
Illustrator:
Jeff Fisher

Client:
Cowley College
Nature of Business:
University art
Design Firm:
Gardner Design
Art Director:
Bill Gardner
Designers:
Bill Gardner, Brian Miller

Client:
Film Foundation of A.A. Bohdziewicz
Nature of Business:
Film foundation
Design Firm:
Atelier Tadeusz Piechura
Art Director:
Tadeusz Piechura
Photographer:
Piotr Tomczyk

RANDOM ACTS *OF SOFTWARE*

Client:
Random Acts of Software
Nature of Business:
Software development
Designer:
Heather Hanly

Client:
Steps With Pets
Nature of Business:
Not-for-profit organization
Design Firm:
Michael Stanard, Inc.
Designer:
Kristy Vandekerckhove
Illustrator:
Kristy Vandekerckhove

Client:
Angela Pezzoni
Nature of Business:
Environmental specialist
Design Firm:
Matite Giovanotte
Designer:
Giovanni Pizzigati

Client:
Red Mountain Park
Nature of Business:
Public park
Design Firm:
DogStar
Art Director:
Greg Hodges/Hodges & Associates
Designer:
Rodney Davidson
Illustrator:
Rodney Davidson

RED MOUNTAIN PARK

Client:
Fat Chance
Nature of Business:
Bird food manufacture
Design Firm:
Gardner Design
Art Director:
Bill Gardner

Client:
Park Preservation Group
Nature of Business:
Park saving and maintenance
Design Firm:
Sommese Design
Art Directors:
Kristin and Lanny Sommese
Designer:
Kristin Sommese
Illustrator:
Lanny Sommese

The Park

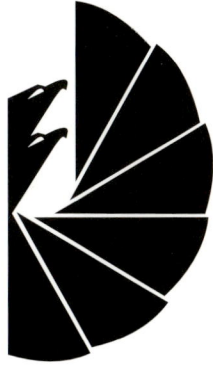

Two Eagles Photo

Client:
Two Eagles Photo
Nature of Business:
Photography
Design Firm:
Gardiner Design
Art Director:
Debi Gardiner
Illustrator:
Debi Gardiner

Client:
St. Louis Cardinals
Nature of Business:
Major league baseball
Design Firm:
Nehman-Kodner Inc.
Art Director:
Gary Kodner

Hobsons Bay
CITY COUNCIL

Client:
Hobsons Bay City Council
Nature of Business:
Local municipality council
Design Firm:
Marcus Lee Design Pty Ltd
Art Director:
Marcus Lee
Designer:
George Margaritis

Client:
Independent School Panthers
Nature of Business:
K-12 School
Design Firm:
Gardner Design
Art Director:
Bill Gardner

Client:
Winnie the Whippet
Nature of Business:
Children celebrity
Design Firm:
Swieter Design Inc.
Art Director:
John Swieter

Client:
Australian Food Merchants
Nature of Business:
Food distribution/export
Design Firm:
Marcus Lee Design Pty Ltd
Art Director:
Marcus Lee
Designer:
George Margaritis

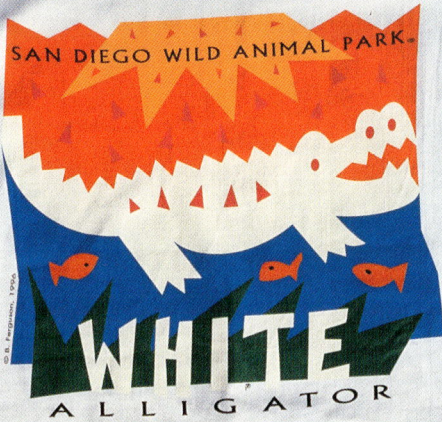

Client:
San Diego Wild Animal Park
Nature of Business:
Zoological society
Design Firm:
Barbara Ferguson Designs
Art Director:
Barbara Ferguson

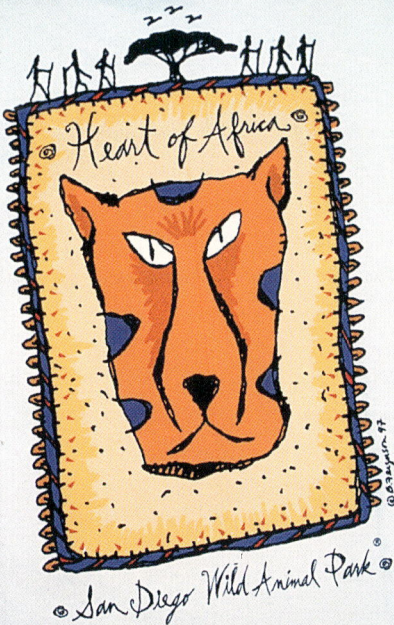

Client:
San Diego Wild Animal Park
Nature of Business:
Zoological society
Design Firm:
Barbara Ferguson Designs
Art Director:
Barbara Ferguson
Illustrator:
Barbara Ferguson

Client:
Aquafuture
Nature of Business:
Indoor Aquaculture facility
Design Firm:
The Wecker Group
Art Director:
Robert J. Wecker

AQUAFUTURE

Client:
CPS Communications
Nature of Business:
Travel information
Design Firm:
Tom Fowler, Inc.
Art Director:
Thomas G. Fowler

CPSCaribnet

Client:
Romora Bay Club
Nature of Business:
Resort/hotel
Design Firm:
Tom Fowler, Inc.
Art Director:
Thomas G. Fowler
Designers:
Thomas G. Fowler, Karl S. Maruyama
Illustrators:
Thomas G. Fowler, Karl S. Maruyama
(computer refinement)

Client:
Wana Zoo
Design Firm:
Supon Design Group
Art Director:
Supon Phornirunlit
Designer:
Sharisse Steber

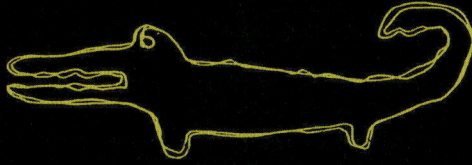

WANA ZOO

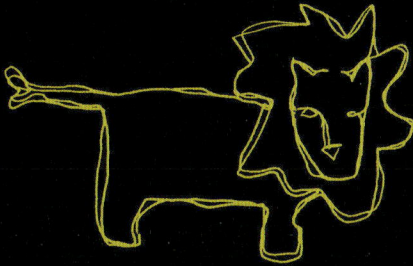

WANA ZOO

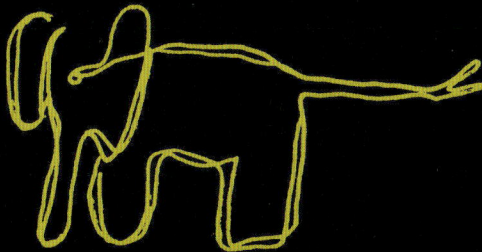

WANA ZOO

Client:
Business Bank of America
Nature of Business:
Financial loans
Design Firm:
Gardner Design
Art Director:
Bill Gardner

Client:
Frankston City Council
Nature of Business:
City municipality council
Design Firm:
Marcus Lee Design Pty Ltd
Art Director:
Marcus Lee
Designer:
George Margaritis

Client:
Cat Jugglers, Inc.
Nature of Business:
Entertainment troupe
Design Firm:
RBMM
Art Director:
Tom Nynas
Illustrator:
Tom Nynas

Client:
Kansas Humane Society
Nature of Business:
Animal shelter
Design Firm:
Gardner Design
Art Director:
Bill Gardner

Client:
Robbers Dog
Nature of Business:
Pub hotel
Design Firm:
Marcus Lee Design Pty Ltd
Art Director:
Marcus Lee

Client:
Australian Drug Foundation
Nature of Business:
Drug and alcohol information
provider
Design Firm:
Marcus Lee Design Pty Ltd
Art Director:
Marcus Lee
Designer:
George Margaritis

Client:
Jane Lee Communications
Nature of Business:
Advertising/public relations
Design Firm:
Greteman Group
Art Director:
Sonia Greteman

Client:
President's Club
Nature of Business:
Travel incentive
Design Firm:
Simple Green In-House Design
Art Director:
Mike Brower
Illustrator:
Tracy Sabin

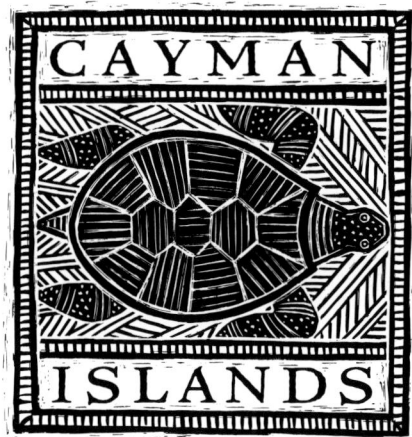

Client:
Wichita Farm and Art Market
Nature of Business:
Old town market building
Design Firm:
Gardner Design
Art Director:
Bill Gardner
Illustrators:
Dave LaFleur, Bill Gardner

Client:
Good Doggie
Design Firm:
Supon Design Group
Art Director:
Supon Phornirunlit
Designer:
Ellen Kim
Illustrator:
Ellen Kim

Client:
Kitty
Design Firm:
Supon Design Group
Art Director:
Supon Phornirunlit
Designer:
Jeanette Nelson

Client:
Jollibee Foods Corporation
Nature of Business:
Fast food
Design Firm:
Addison Design Consultants Pte Ltd
Art Directors:
Margaret Widelock, Sarah Lewis-Smith
Designers:
Julia Ng, Nic Ng
Illustrator:
Einstein

Jollibee.

Patricia S. Roxas
Marketing Manager, Products

Jollibee.

Jollibee Foods Corporation
P.O. Box 12695 Ortigas Center
Pasig City 1600, Philippines
7/F Jollibee Center, San Miguel Avenue
Pasig, Metro Manila, Philippines
Tel (632) 634 1111 Fax (632) 634 1191
Pager (123) WORK HD

Jollibee.

Jollibee Foods Corporation PO Box 12695 Ortigas Center, Pasig City 1600, Philippines
5/F Jollibee Center, San Miguel Avenue, Pasig, Metro Manila, Philippines Tel (632) 634 1111 Fax (632) 635 8868

Client:
Pet Fair
Nature of Business:
Trade show
Design Firm:
Sheehan Design
Art Director:
Jamie Sheehan
Photographer:
Michels Studio
Printer:
The Allied Printers

645 SOUTHCENTER MALL
SUITE #341
SEATTLE, WA 98188
(206) 559-4524

TIMOTHY ENARSON, EVENT COORDINATOR

645 SOUTHCENTER MALL
SUITE #341
SEATTLE, WA 98188
(206) 559-4524

645 SOUTHCENTER MALL · SUITE #341 · SEATTLE, WA 98188

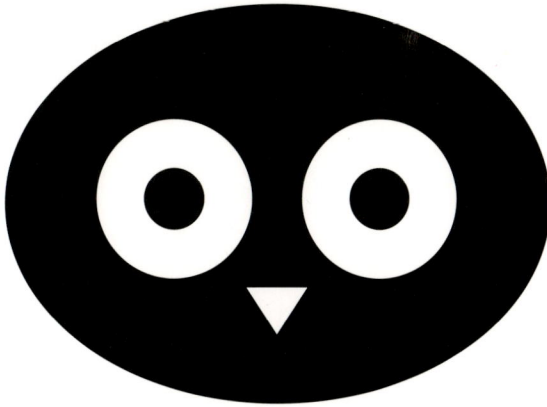

Client:
Night Owl Security
Nature of Business:
Residential security
Design Firm:
Pat Taylor, Inc.
Art Director:
Pat Taylor
Illustrator:
Graphics X Gallo

HOOCH & HOLLY'S

Client:
Hooch + Holly's
Nature of Business:
Restaurant
Design Firm:
Korn Design
Art Director:
Denise Korn
Designer:
Javier Cortés
Illustrator:
Jenny Pelzek

Client:
Advanced Cardiovascular Systems
Nature of Business:
Medical supplies
Design Firm:
Tracy Sabin Graphic Design
Art Director:
Scott Mires
Illustrator:
Tracy Sabin

Client:
DogStar
Nature of Business:
Design
Design Firm:
DogStar
Designer:
Rodney Davidson
Illustrator:
Rodney Davidson

PAST DUE

Client:
DogStar
Nature of Business:
Design
Design Firm:
DogStar
Designer:
Rodney Davidson
Illustrator:
Rodney Davidson

PAST DUE

Client:
DogStar
Nature of Business:
Design
Design Firm:
DogStar
Designer:
Rodney Davidson
Illustrator:
Rodney Davidson

PAST DUE

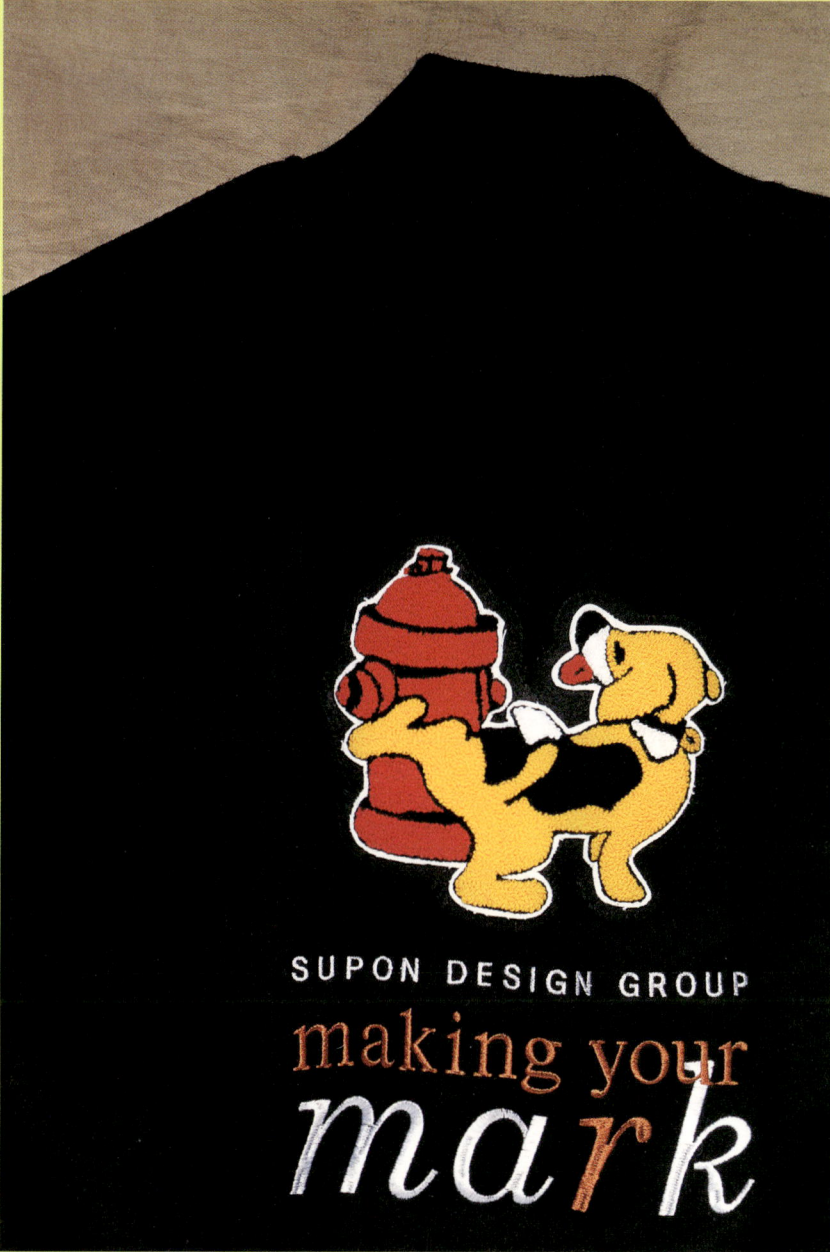

Client:
Supon Design Group
Nature of business:
Graphic Design
Design Firm:
Supon Design Group
Art Director:
Supon Phornirunlit
Designer:
Khoi Vinh

Client:
Phoenix Capital Management
Nature of Business:
Financial consulting
Design Firm:
Eclipse
Art Director:
Byron Jacobs
Illustrators:
Byron Jacobs, Chris Chan

Client:
Zoological Society of San Diego
Nature of Business:
Zoo
Design Firm:
Zoological Society of San Diego
Art Director:
Tim Reamer

Client:
Bruce and Sue Mullins
Nature of Business:
Private yacht
Design Firm:
Eclipse
Art Director:
Byron Jacobs
Illustrator:
Byron Jacobs

Client:
Epic Cycling
Nature of Business:
Mountain bike event
Design Firm:
RealWorld Media
Art Director:
Kevin Raffler
Designers:
Kevin Raffler, Wes Wickham
Illustrators:
Kevin Raffler, Wes Wickham

Client:
Hot Rod Hell
Nature of Business:
Custom car shop
Design Firm:
Mires Design, Inc.
Art Director:
José Serrano
Illustrator:
Tracy Sabin

Client:
Supon Design Group
Nature of business:
Graphic design
Design Firm:
Supon Design Group
Art Director:
Supon Phornirunlit
Designer:
Rodney Davidson

Client:
Hand Real Estate
Nature of Business:
Commercial real estate
Design Firm:
Pat Taylor, Inc.
Art Director:
Pat Taylor
Illustrator:
Graphics X Gallo

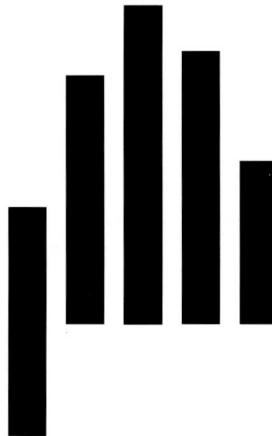

Client:
Glory
Nature of Business:
Hand made recycled clothing
Design Firm:
Gardner Design
Art Director:
Bill Gardner
Designers:
Bill Gardner, Karen Hogan

Client:
Strategic Change Management
Nature of Business:
Marketing consulting
Design Firm:
After Hours Creative
Art Director:
After Hours Creative

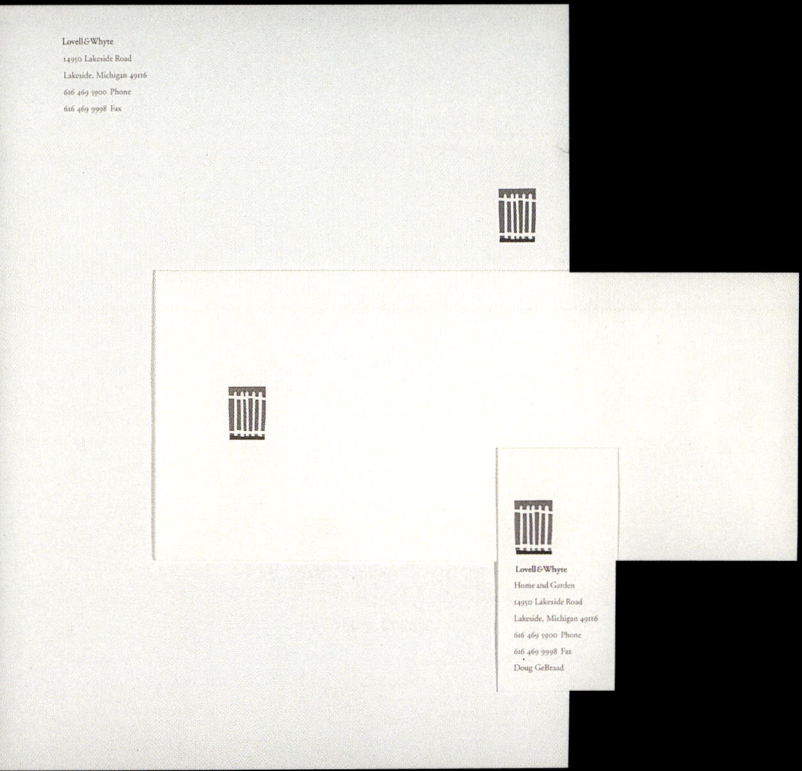

Client:
Lovell + Whyte
Nature of Business:
Retail home and garden furnishings
Design Firm:
Kym Abrams Design
Art Director:
Kym Abrams
Designer:
Amy Nathan
Illustrator:
Amy Nathan

Client:
Fuseworks
Nature of Business:
Internet game platform
Design Firm:
Parable Communications Corp.
Art Director:
David Craib
Printer:
M.O.M. Printing

Client:
Hornall Anderson Design Works, Inc.
Nature of Business:
Graphic design
Design Firm:
Hornall Anderson Design Works, Inc.
Art Director:
Jack Anderson
Designers:
Jack Anderson, David Bates
Illustrator:
David Bates

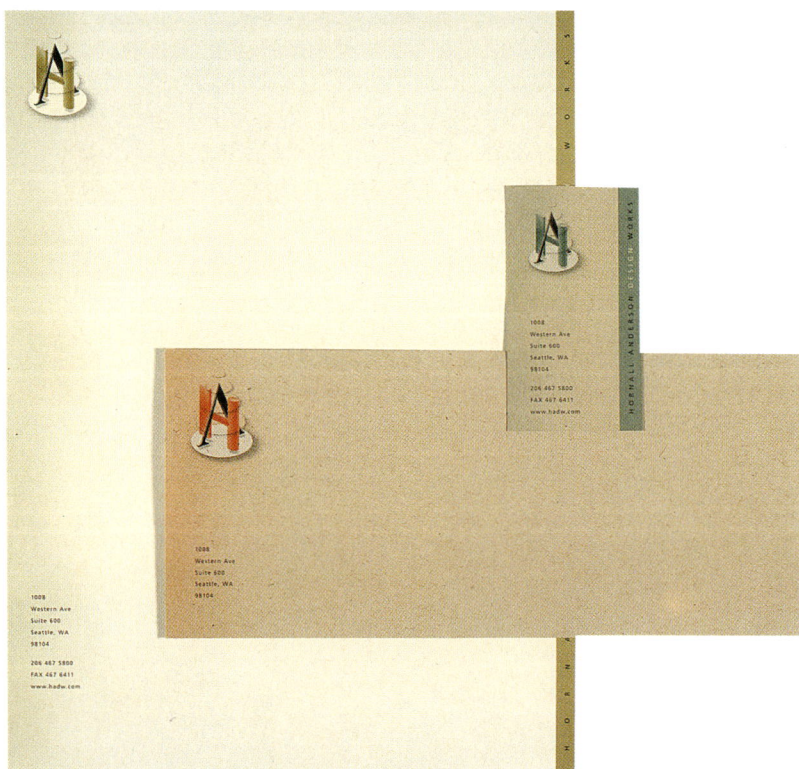

Labatt

ICE

allez up

X-Tension.com

Client:
Labatt Breweries Inc.
Nature of Business:
Brewer
Design Firm:
Tarzan Communications Inc.
Art Directors:
Daniel Fortin, George Fok
Designers:
George Fok, Daniel Fortin
Illustrator:
George Fok

Client:
Allez Up
Nature of Business:
Indoor climbing gym
Design Firm:
Robert Beck Design
Art Director:
Robert Beck

Client:
XTension.com
Nature of Business:
On-line Quark extensions
Design Firm:
Bruce Yelaska Design
Art Director:
Bruce Yelaska

Client:
Cafe Go
Nature of Business:
Coffee/take-out cafe
Design Firm:
Bruce Yelaska Design
Art Director:
Bruce Yelaska

Client:
Sweet Vanilla
Nature of Business:
Ice cream parlor
Design Firm:
Interface Designers
Art Director:
Silvana Mattievich

Client:
Aspen Bagel and Brew
Nature of Business:
Bagel and coffee shop
Design Firm:
Fuszion Art + Design
Art Director:
Richard Lee Hefner
Designers:
Michael Pfister, Richard Lee Hefner
Illustrator:
Mike Pfister

Client:
CW Gourmet/Mondeo
Nature of Business:
Restaurant
Design Firm:
Hornall Anderson Design Works, Inc.
Art Director:
Jack Anderson
Designers:
Jack Anderson, David Bates,
Sonja Max
Illustrator:
David Bates

INDEX BY DESIGN FIRM

INDEX BY DESIGN FIRM

INDEX BY CLIENT

INDEX BY CLIENT

INDEX BY CLIENT